CAREERS FOR
LEGAL EAGLES
& Other
Law-and-Order Types

W9-AXZ-337

VGM Careers for You Series

CAREERS FOR

LEGAL EAGLES

& Other
Law-and-Order Types

Blythe Camenson

VGM Career Horizons
NTC/Contemporary Publishing Group

Library of Congress Cataloging-in-Publication Data

Camenson, Blythe.
    Careers for legal eagles & other law-and-order types / Blythe Camenson.
       p.   cm.—(VGM careers for you series)
    ISBN 0-8442-2288-7 (cloth)
    ISBN 0-8442-2289-5 (paper)
    1. Law—Vocational guidance—United States.   I. Title.
II. Series.
KF297.Z9C358   1998
340'.023'73—dc21   97-46614
                                           CIP

Published by VGM Career Horizons
A division of NTC/Contemporary Publishing Group, Inc.
4255 West Touhy Avenue, Lincolnwood (Chicago), Illinois 60646-1975 U.S.A.
Copyright © 1998 by NTC/Contemporary Publishing Group, Inc.
All rights reserved. No part of this book may be reproduced, stored in a retrieval
system, or transmitted in any form or by any means, electronic, mechanical,
photocopying, recording, or otherwise, without the prior written permission of
NTC/Contemporary Publishing Group, Inc.
Printed in the United States of America
International Standard Book Number: 0-8442-2288-7 (cloth)
                                     0-8442-2289-5 (paper)
99 00 01 02 03 04 VP 20 19 18 17 16 15 14 13 12 11 10 9 8 7 6 5 4 3 2

To Sara Goodman, my friend and favorite legal eagle.

Contents

Acknowledgments

The author would like to thank the following legal eagles for providing information about their careers:

Barbara F. Arrants	Public Defender
Timothy Bronson	Detective Sergeant
Matthew Carone	Gallery Owner/Forgery Investigator
Dan P. Clark	Court Reporter
Kimberly Diehl	Jailer
Mike W. Elliott	Assistant District Attorney
Gist Fleshman	Clerk of the Court
Jennifer Franks	Legal Secretary
Chris Goodwin	Investigator
M. J. Goodwin	Family Law
Barbara Grace Lake	Legal Assistant
James Lanuti	Circuit Court Judge
Joe Nickell	Undercover Investigator
Ramesh Nyberg	Homicide Detective
Kent Reeves	Bailiff
Timothy T. Speed Jr.	Security Supervisor
Gigi Starnes	Legal Secretary
Joseph Tringali	Assistant State Attorney General
John Wiorek	Law Clerk

CHAPTER ONE

Options for Legal Eagles

C rime doesn't pay, they say, but that old saw is aimed at criminals. On the other side of the law, there is a vast array of careers for law-abiding and justice-seeking individuals—and they all offer legitimate paychecks.

But there's no room for armchair concerned citizens here. Any of the careers covered in this book can have you out where the action is. Some of the work is detail oriented, some is frustrating, and some involves danger—but there's no greater reward than tracking down real criminals, prosecuting them, and seeing justice at work.

Perhaps you're concerned that the only route to a career in law is the long haul—years and years of law school, bar exams, and stiff competition for jobs with the best firms. It's true, most lawyers go through that. But there are many other paths to follow that can lead you to an exciting law-related career. Have a look at the following overview of career areas from which you can choose, then read on to see what they involve.

Jobs for Legal Eagles

Attorneys at Law

F. Lee Bailey, Robert Shapiro, and Johnnie Cochran aside, Perry Mason is probably the best-known lawyer in this country. His clients are always innocent, he always gets them off, and he always nabs the real criminal in the process.

But real life does not always follow the imagination of television writers. For every F. Lee Bailey, there's a Marcia Clark, for every Mason, a Burger. If you decide to pursue a career in criminal law, many of your clients will not be innocent, and you might not be able to get all of them acquitted. Some you'd even rather not represent. But, in our justice system, everyone is innocent until proven guilty, and everyone is entitled to legal defense.

Criminal lawyers operate their own practices, work for private law firms, or represent clients under the auspices of the Public Defender's Office. Lawyers who work for state attorneys general, prosecutors, and courts play a key role in the criminal justice system. At the federal level, attorneys investigate cases for the Department of Justice or other agencies. Also, lawyers at every government level help develop programs, draft laws, interpret legislation, establish enforcement procedures, and argue civil and criminal cases on behalf of the government.

But criminal trial work is not the only option open to lawyers. Just as doctors can gear their careers toward a particular specialty, so can lawyers. Chapter 2 will introduce you to a variety of law specializations.

Judges

Judges apply the law. They oversee the legal process that, in courts of law, resolves civil disputes and determines guilt in criminal cases according to federal and state laws and those of local jurisdictions.

They preside over cases touching on virtually every aspect of society, from traffic offenses to disputes over management of professional sports, from the rights of huge corporations to questions of disconnecting life support equipment for terminally ill patients. Judges must ensure that trials and hearings are conducted fairly and that the court administers justice in a manner that safeguards the legal rights of all parties involved.

Although not all judges have been lawyers first, most have been to law school and have worked as practicing attorneys. Chapter 3 will introduce you to this demanding career.

Court Staff

With access to Court TV and so many media-grabbing trials finding their way to the airwaves, most people have become familiar with the different personnel who make up the court staff. You've seen the judge and the bailiff and the court reporter. But there are others who work behind the scenes—in jobs that might be just right for you. See Chapter 4 for an inside look at courtroom life.

Paralegals

Not all legal work requires a law degree. Lawyers are often assisted in their work by paralegals, who are also known as legal assistants. Paralegals perform many of the same tasks as lawyers, except for those tasks considered to be the practice of law.

Paralegals can enter this exciting field through a formal training program or, sometimes, be trained on the job. In Chapter 5 you'll meet an experienced paralegal who has a lot to say about this particular job path.

Legal Secretaries

Most organizations employ secretaries to perform and coordinate office activities and to ensure that information gets disseminated in a timely fashion to staff and clients. Managers, professionals, and other support staff rely on legal secretaries to keep administrative operations under control. Their specific duties depend upon their level of responsibility and the type of firm in which they are employed. See Chapter 6 for more information on this field.

Law Enforcement Officers

The safety of our nation's cities, towns, and highways greatly depends on the work of police officers, deputy sheriffs, detectives, and special agents whose responsibilities range from controlling traffic to preventing and investigating crimes. In Chapter 7 you'll learn all about the various paths open to you in law enforcement.

Private Investigators

Fancy yourself a Magnum, P.I., type, or maybe another Kinsey Milhone, Sue Grafton's star detective? The field of private investigation can be exciting and glamorous; it can also be tedious and dull. For every undercover operation, there are hundreds of hours spent on the telephone or surfing the Net, and an equal number sitting in a car at a stakeout, cupping a mug of cold coffee. Chapter 8 will give you an inside look at what it's really like to work in private investigation.

Corrections Officers

Corrections officers are charged with the security and safety of persons who have been arrested, who are awaiting trials or other hearings, or who have been convicted and sentenced to serve time in a correctional institution. You have probably never been in a jail or prison. Do the movies portray life there accurately? You'll meet a real-life prison guard in Chapter 9—she'll fill you in.

Security Guards

Security guards work in a variety of settings, and often the work is routine, dull even. But every once in a while, a security guard remembers why he or she was hired—and for the off chance of something going wrong, you have to be prepared. Learn more about this field from a security guard in Chapter 10.

Choosing Your Field

People who work in law careers give of themselves in many different capacities, providing valuable service to their communities. If you're reading this book, chances are you're already considering a career in one of the many areas of this wide-open field.

But perhaps you're not sure of the working conditions the different fields offer or which area would suit your personality, skills, and lifestyle the most. There are several factors to consider when deciding which sector to pursue. Each field carries with it different levels of responsibility and commitment. To identify occupations that will match your expectations, you need to know what each job entails.

Ask yourself the following questions and make note of your answers. Then, as you go through the following chapters, compare your requirements to the information provided by the professionals interviewed inside. Their comments will help you pinpoint the fields that would interest you and eliminate those that would clearly be the wrong choice.

- How much time are you willing to commit to training? Some skills can be learned on the job or in a year or two of formal training; others can take considerably longer.

- Do you want to work in an office behind a desk or would you prefer to be out and about, patrolling a beat or meeting with clients in their homes—or in prison?

- Can you handle a certain amount of stress on the job, or would you prefer a quiet—and safe—environment?

- How much money do you expect to earn starting out and after you have a few years' experience under your belt? Salaries and earnings vary greatly for each profession.

- How much independence do you require? Do you want to be your own boss or will you be content as a salaried employee?

- Would you rather work daytime hours or would you prefer evenings and weekends?

- Can you pay attention to detail and handle paperwork, legal documents, and reports?

Knowing what your expectations are, then comparing them to the realities of the work, will help you make informed choices.

The Training You'll Need

The training required for the various law and law-related careers varies greatly. Some positions are entry level, requiring no more than a high school education. Some demand that you be physically fit and have some prior work experience. Others require specific skills and from two to four years of college or a technical training program. Still others require several years of postgraduate study after earning your bachelor's degree.

Resources are listed throughout each chapter to tell you about job requirements and avenues for education and/or on-the-job training.

For More Information

In the Appendix you will find professional associations for many of the career paths explored in this book. Most offer booklets and pamphlets with career information; some are free, others might have a nominal charge of one or two dollars. A phone call or letter will have information in the mail to you within a few days.

CHAPTER TWO

Attorneys at Law

T he more detailed aspects of a lawyer's job depend upon his or her position and field of specialization. Even though all lawyers are allowed to represent parties in court, some appear in court more frequently than others. Lawyers who specialize in trial work need an exceptional ability to think quickly and speak with ease and authority, and they must be thoroughly familiar with courtroom rules and strategies. Trial lawyers still spend most of their time outside the courtroom conducting research, interviewing clients and witnesses, and handling other details in preparation for trial.

Specializations

Besides trial courts, lawyers practice law in a variety of places. The majority are in private practice, but specializations in other areas of law exist for those interested in legal careers.

Lawyers

Lawyers can work for large or small firms, operate their own private practices, or represent clients as public defenders. They work in either criminal or civil law or both.

Criminal Law

In criminal law, lawyers represent individuals who have been charged with crimes and argue their cases in courts of law.

Civil Law

In civil law, attorneys assist clients with litigation, wills, trusts, contracts, mortgages, titles, and leases. Some manage a person's property as trustee or, as executor, see that provisions of a client's will are carried out. Others handle only public-interest cases, civil or criminal, that have a potential impact extending well beyond the individual client.

Other lawyers work for legal aid societies—private, nonprofit organizations established to serve disadvantaged people. These lawyers generally handle civil rather than criminal cases.

Some other specializations within civil law include:

- bankruptcy

- environmental law

- family law

- insurance law

- intellectual property

- international law

- probate

- public defense

- real estate law

House Counsel

Lawyers sometimes are employed full-time by a single client. If the client is a corporation, the lawyer is known as *house counsel* and usually advises the company about legal questions that arise from its business activities. These questions might involve patents, government regulations, contracts with other companies, property interests, or collective-bargaining agreements with unions.

Government Attorneys

Attorneys employed at the various levels of government make up still another category of legal practitioners. Lawyers who work for state attorneys general, prosecutors, public defenders, and courts play key roles in the criminal justice system. At the federal level, attorneys investigate cases for the U.S. Department of Justice or other agencies. Also, lawyers at every government level help develop programs, draft laws, interpret legislation, establish enforcement procedures, and argue civil and criminal cases on behalf of the government.

Law Clerks

Law clerks are fully trained attorneys who choose to work with a judge, either for a one- to two-year stint out of law school to gain experience before practicing law or as a full-time professional career. Their duties involve mainly research and writing reports.

Law Professors

A relatively small number of trained attorneys work in law schools. Most are faculty members who specialize in one or more subjects, and others serve as administrators. Some work full-time in nonacademic settings and teach part-time.

Working Conditions for Legal Eagles

Lawyers and judges do most of their work in offices, law libraries, and courtrooms. Lawyers sometimes meet in clients' homes or places of business and, when necessary, in hospitals or prisons. They frequently travel to attend meetings; to gather evidence; and to appear before courts, legislative bodies, and other authorities.

Salaried lawyers in government and private corporations generally have structured work schedules. Lawyers in private practice may work irregular hours while conducting research, conferring with clients, or preparing briefs during nonoffice hours.

Lawyers often work long hours, and about half of all practicing lawyers regularly work fifty hours or more per week. They are under particularly heavy pressure, for example, when a case is being tried. Although work generally is not seasonal, the work of tax lawyers and other specialists may be an exception. Because lawyers in private practice can often determine their own workloads and when they will retire, many stay in practice well beyond the usual retirement age.

No matter the setting, whether acting as advocate or prosecutor, all attorneys interpret the law and apply it to specific situations. This requires research and communication abilities. Preparation for court includes keeping abreast of the latest laws and judicial decisions.

Lawyers perform in-depth research into the purposes behind the applicable laws and into judicial decisions that have been applied to those laws under circumstances similar to those currently faced by the client. While all lawyers make use of law libraries to prepare cases, some supplement their searches of the conventional printed sources with computer software packages that automatically search the legal literature and identify legal texts that may be relevant to a specific subject.

In litigation that involves many supporting documents, lawyers may also use computers to organize and index the material. Lawyers then communicate to others the information obtained by research.

What It's Really Like

Barbara F. Arrants—Public Defender

Barbara Arrants earned her B.S. in psychology in 1985 from the University of the South in Sewanee, Tennessee, and her J.D. from the University of Tennessee, Knoxville, in 1991.

"I worked for four years for the Davidson County Metropolitan Public Defender's Office in Nashville, Tennessee. I started as a general sessions attorney, handling misdemeanor trials and bind-over hearings, then worked as a criminal court attorney (felony trials), then I was named lead trial attorney for DUI court, which covered DUI (driving under the influence), vehicular homicide, and aggravated assault trials and hearings.

"One of the first things I ever did at the public defender's office was investigate a triple homicide. I had to review the crime scene photos, autopsies, and then do extensive interviews with the defendant and his family. I could've written a book on how to create a killer!

"A public defender's life is thrilling, exciting, stressful, thankless, impossible, and wonderful—all rolled into one. I worked forty-five to fifty-five hours a week. As a general sessions attorney I would walk into court every morning, court docket in hand, with some fifteen to twenty-five names highlighted. These were my clients for the day, many of whom I would meet for the first time in court. Needless to say, you have to be able to think on your feet. I would meet and talk with each of my clients for a few minutes, then go into the courtroom for the call of the docket. After docket call, I met with the district attorneys. As a result of this meeting, I marked some cases for trial, some for a bond-reduction hearing, some for plea-bargain offers, and some for bind-over hearings. I stayed in court all day until all of the cases were disposed of. I handled all of the hearings, trials, and pleas that day. This goes on every day, five days a week. All of the trials are bench trials (judge only) unless the client requests otherwise. If a client requests a jury trial, the case is bound over to the grand jury.

"Criminal court is not quite so hectic, but the cases are more serious and the trials are almost always in front of a jury. I was actually in court about three days a week: two days for trials, sometimes longer, and one day for motions and hearings. I handled every aspect of a client's felony case: arraignment, research, investigation, pretrial motions, bond issues, and trial.

"DUI court was the same. I handled DUIs set for jury trial (i.e., they were not settled or tried in general sessions court), vehicular homicide, and aggravated assault (with a vehicle). As DUI attorney I was in charge of approximately two hundred active cases, including probation violations. I was in court two to three days a week for trials, hearings, and motions. I averaged one jury trial per week.

"The work atmosphere in public defense is high pressure, confrontational, and intense, but very exciting. What I liked most was the enormous amount of courtroom work. If you like litigation, it's the place to be.

"What I disliked was fighting the stereotype that P.D.s are lousy lawyers simply because they work for indigent clients. In fact, in most cases, the opposite is true. Most of the P.D.s I know are exceptional attorneys. Like me, they graduated in the top part of their class and do this type of work because they enjoy it, not because they couldn't get any other job.

"The main difference between a P.D. and a hired attorney is the amount of money available for expert witnesses, tests, exhibits, and the like. The other difference is the huge workload a public defender handles. A private attorney will have one client for the day; I may have twenty! The quality of the attorney is essentially the same, however.

"I am no longer working as a public defender. I am in private practice now, but truthfully I am home with young children. I will return to criminal practice full-time in a few years. I found it very difficult to keep up the relentless pace of P.D. work and be a mother. Sometimes I would have to go across town in the middle of the night for an interview, or downtown to the Criminal Justice Center for a lineup or interrogation. I decided that while my children were young, I needed to stay home for a few years. I really miss the work, but it was difficult on my family."

How Barbara Arrants Got Started

"I went to law school because—let's face it—a liberal arts degree means I have a good education but no qualifications for anything. While applying for law school and taking the LSATs, I worked as a runner for a large firm here in Nashville. I became acquainted with all the different types of law there are, what one actually *did* as a lawyer, and so forth. I came away with the feeling that I did not want to be an associate in a firm. All associates do is the partners' paperwork. That did not appeal to me at all. I wanted to be in the thick of things!

"During my first year at law school I attended the mock trial competition (held every year in every law school nationwide). That's all it took. I took a trial advocacy course my second year and blew my professor away—got the highest grade in the class. He told me that litigation was where I needed to be.

"Criminal law appeals to me because of my psychology background—what makes people do the things they do? Why does someone become a criminal? I could have been a prosecutor or a defense attorney—I fell into the defense side simply because someone told me the P.D.s were always looking for interns. I interned with public defense and was offered a job before I had finished my second year. Never one to look a gift horse in the mouth, I jumped on it."

Sound Advice from Barbara Arrants

"If you are interested in litigation, a job as a public defender or district attorney gets you more experience at a faster pace than any other career choice. If you start your career with a firm, you can expect to wait as long as five years before you see the inside of a courtroom. I handled my first bench trial the first week I was working! It is incredibly demanding, but very rewarding as well."

Joseph Tringali—Assistant State Attorney General

Joseph Tringali has been an attorney since 1970. He earned both his B.A. in history and his J.D. at the State University of New York, Buffalo. He joined the staff of the attorney general's office in Palm Beach County, Florida, in 1990.

"The attorney general of any state is the chief law officer of the state. In Florida in the attorney general's office there are probably two hundred assistant attorneys general in offices in various cities statewide. We represent the state in civil actions, such as the big tobacco lawsuit that's going on now.

"I'm not involved in that, though. I handle criminal appeals on behalf of the state. When these criminals, who are convicted beyond a reasonable doubt and are sent off to prison, where they richly deserve to be, appeal and attempt to get out, it's my job to keep them in.

"In some states the local prosecutors have an appellate division in each office. Our state has elected the system of having all appellate cases handled by the attorney general.

"Although my job title is different, I function similarly to prosecuting attorneys. In New York state, for example, I was an assistant district attorney and our office handled both prosecuting cases and the appeals.

"Appellate law is a much more esoteric practice and much less stressful than trial law. In a trial situation you are the key player, especially if you are the prosecutor. It's up to you to have the witnesses there on time; it's up to you call them in the order you need them. You're the maestro—you're conducting the orchestra.

"In my job I'm in court very rarely. Generally speaking, I handle a lot of drug cases, a lot of homicide cases. The appellant is bringing the action, so the first thing that happens is that I get a brief from the defendant's attorney, who argues that there were all these legal errors at the trial. I read the brief, then I might spend one to three days reading the transcript of the trial, looking to see if things happened they way the defense attorney said they did. Sometimes things can be interpreted differently. Then I'll research the case law, other appellate cases on those legal issues. Then I write a brief in opposition, called an *answer brief,* on behalf of the state. The appellant gets to write what is called a *reply brief.* Then all the briefs get filed in the appellate court.

The appellate judge and his or her law clerks then study all the briefs. Although my position is similar to that of a law clerk working with an appellate judge, he or she is supposed to be impartial. I'm an advocate for the state. The law clerk is neutral; I'm trying to find ways to uphold the conviction.

"After the judge goes over the briefs, 90 percent of the time nothing else happens. The appellate court will either affirm the conviction without comment or will write an opinion either affirming or reversing the original judgment. If it gets reversed, usually it means that the state has to retry the case.

"Every once in a while, one side or the other will request an oral argument. That's when we get to go to court and give an oral presentation. There's a great difference of opinion on whether oral arguments actually do the appellant any good. During my first oral argument I was in there heating up the courtroom, with the old trial lawyer instincts coming out, and one of the judges said to me, 'Counselor, you can relax. There's no jury here.' In other words, there's nobody to impress here with theatrics. The judges know the law and all you need to do is make your point intelligently and then sit down. I get to make an oral argument maybe once a month or once every six weeks. It's the part of my work I enjoy the most.

"I honestly prefer the work I'm doing now as opposed to trial lawyering. This is the pure practice of law without the personalities or the peculiarities of any particular trial judge. You don't have to worry about whether witnesses will show up or whether they'll be good or bad witnesses. When you're a prosecuting attorney it feels more like playing *Let's Make a Deal.* It's easy to get burned out.

"My job is law as an intellectual exercise."

How Joseph Tringali Got Started

"I was always interested in the idea of government and I was attracted by trial law in particular, the drama of the courtroom. Maybe I should have been an actor. This was the era of *Perry Mason*, and everyone saw that on television. But I also spent quite a bit of time in downtown Buffalo when I was in high school and even later when I was in college. I would go into the courthouse and actually watch the trials as they were going on. And of course the reality is a lot different from *Perry Mason*. I would hang around and see the lawyers rushing to and fro in the hallways. Probably the most dramatic scenes take place there rather than in the courtrooms. That's where the lawyers are huddling with their clients and explaining the facts of legal life.

"After I graduated law school, I worked in Buffalo as an assistant district attorney for two years, then I came down to Palm Beach County in Florida as an assistant state attorney. It was the same job as in New York but with a different title. I stayed for three years then went back to Buffalo and worked as assistant corporation counsel for two years, representing the city of Buffalo and doing labor law cases. Then I went into private practice for fourteen years, handling all sorts of cases—criminal, family—anything that came through the door.

"In 1990 I came back to Florida and took my present job working for the attorney general."

Sound Advice from Joseph Tringali

"Law is a much more demanding profession than most people realize. I think that anyone who enters it should be aware that it is not the *Perry Mason*, television/movie kind of thing. Nor is it the high-income profession everyone thinks it is across the board. Yes, there are a lot of attorneys out there earning a lot of money. But there are also attorneys running themselves

ragged from courtroom to courtroom earning less than I do—
and I earn only $45,500 a year.

"Don't go out and buy the Mercedes just yet."

Mike W. Elliott—Assistant District Attorney

Mike Elliott works in the Fort Bend County District Attorney's
Office in Richmond, Texas, approximately thirty miles south-
west of Houston.

"I truly enjoy my job and enjoy each and every day at work.
The majority of my time is either spent in court prosecuting the
bad guys or getting ready for the next trial. Each day brings a
new challenge. The average work week is approximately sixty
hours.

"I love the feeling of getting a bad guy off the streets. I hate
seeing someone who gets locked up only to get out of prison
early because of parole only to revictimize someone else.

"As a prosecuting attorney, I feel I can make a difference in
today's society. I sleep well at night knowing that my actions
help to make our society a safer place to live and raise our
children."

Mike Elliott's Background

Mike Elliott earned his B.A. in political science from the
University of Texas at Arlington in 1989 and his J.D. from
Houston's South Texas College of Law in 1991. He has worked
in the D.A.'s office since 1992.

Some Expert Advice from Mike Elliott

"If you want to be a lawyer, you should look inside yourself and
examine your motives. If it is for money or prestige, my advice
would be to embark upon another profession. There are too

many greedy lawyers already. However, if you want to help the world and society with skills such as prosecuting, then I highly recommend the profession."

M. J. Goodwin—Family Law

M. J. Goodwin has a B.A. in modern languages and a minor in business from Clemson University in South Carolina. She received her J.D. from the University of South Carolina in Columbia in 1991.

"I am a female solo practitioner, which makes me a minority in my town, Anderson, South Carolina. My firm has three employees: my husband, who left his job this year to join my firm as my manager/investigator, my paralegal, and me. I've been open almost two years and have done better than I ever imagined I would. I envisioned starving to death. But that hasn't happened.

"I practice in a variety of areas. If I had to guess, I would say it's about 80 percent family law (divorce, custody, adoption, guardianships), 15 percent personal injury (wrecks, worker's compensation, and so on), and 5 percent of whatever comes in the door that I think I can handle. I do no real estate or tax work—boring stuff to me . . . plus, it makes malpractice insurance higher.

"I am basically a trial lawyer. I don't like to be still or sit in the office too much.

"I now also have a part-time contract as the city prosecutor, which means I handle municipal level crimes for our local public defender, mainly DUI and some domestic violence or an occasional shoplifter.

"There is no such thing as a typical day in my practice. It all depends on what kind of fire you have to put out. With domestic litigation, divorces, child custody, separations, adoptions, anything in family court—any time you're dealing with somebody's family, particularly the breakup of a marriage or a custody dispute—well, these are the most emotionally charged kind of cases. I did murder cases as a prosecutor, but these are worse than a murder case. These people are to some extent more torn up than a murder victim's family is. It's real hard to deal with people who are thinking with their emotions—and they don't realize they're doing it. They're so hurt they can't think straight. And that's what makes it stressful. Even when they win, and we have a pretty high success rate, they don't feel any better. The legal win doesn't heal the emotional scar. And I think that comes as a shock to them.

"I run around a lot, going to meeting with clients, going to court almost every day, doing a lot of paperwork—summonses and complaints and answers and counterclaims and affidavits and financial declarations. This is very busy, and it's different from other civil litigation because there's so much contact with the client. If you get a car-wreck case, the client comes in and you get the medical report and take the deposition and maybe have one or two meetings. But with domestic clients, they're in almost every day because they're so upset. If they have children, it's particularly difficult for them to separate themselves from their spouses—there's always visitations and exchanges and there's always some kind of fussing going on there.

"I prefer being on my own rather than working for a large firm because it gives me more control. If I don't have to go to court or if I don't have an appointment, I can stay home until ten-thirty or eleven o'clock if I want to. I'm in charge. The flip side of that, though, is that I'm responsible for everything. If something needs to be done Saturday night, I'm going to be the one to do it.

"There's a lot of satisfaction in helping people. The legal system is real complicated, and helping people get through that, however it's going to be resolved, is rewarding. Not everyone gets a good verdict; not everyone wins.

"I do a lot of pro bono cases. When I left the prosecutor's office I made a public commitment to try to continue helping battered women. I called the newspapers and told them I would help women who were staying in the shelter, that I would cut my hourly rate and let them make payments. I think that once someone has gone to the shelter she's made enough of a commitment to get out. I had prosecuted these cases before. I think I can help more now. So many of these women refuse to prosecute; they just want to get away. So I try to help with their divorces. But you have a horrible problem with a lot of them going back into the marriages. Everyone's got to have a cause. This is my torch.

"If I had been asked three years ago when I was at the prosecutor's office, I probably would have said I was really unhappy and wished that I hadn't gone to law school. I was actually thinking that way at that time. I enjoyed the work, I was still helping people, but there's a high burnout rate in prosecuting or even in defending.

"Burnout is caused by the high volume of cases pending all at the same time, the nature of the work (dealing with victimized souls and putting up with criminals), and the very low pay (as compared to private practice and larger firms). As an example on the pay, look at O.J. Simpson's trial. Marcia Clark earned around $90,000 a year. O.J.'s defense team got millions from one trial. That is certainly an extreme, but even with my part-time job, there is a huge discrepancy. Prosecutors can't afford to put on as good a case as a well-funded defendant.

"A prosecutor has so many bosses to please: the immediate supervisor, the judge, the public, the victim, and the police. It's unlikely that you can please them all at the same time. And the criminal justice system is so far behind. It can take forever to get to trial. That adds to the frustration.

"And prosecutors are almost always in the spotlight, even in a small town. I can remember being in the paper and on TV a lot, and I found that stressful.

"But now I'm very happy. It's very different to be your own boss."

How M. J. Goodwin Got Started

"I was all set to go on and get a master's in French, and then I was called for jury duty and I was absolutely fascinated, mesmerized. After that I started sending to law schools for information. I was a junior at Clemson at the time. Law school will take any major, so I didn't have to change mine.

"Straight out of law school I worked as an assistant prosecutor. I handled juveniles, domestic violence, and some sex crimes, particularly those involving children, for about three years. In September of 1994 I opened my own firm."

Expert Advice from M. J. Goodwin

"Don't do this with the idea you're going to get rich. It's a big misconception. The prosecutor jobs around here, for example, pay between $32,000 and $40,000 a year. You can make more working in a big bank. The large firms pay very well, but they expect sixty to seventy-five hours a week.

"In my solo practice, how I get paid depends on what kind of case it is. For domestic work I charge by the hour—my fee is $100 an hour—because contingency fees in divorce cases are prohibited by our code of ethics. You wouldn't want an attorney pushing someone not to settle a case so they could get a bigger fee. For some cases, such as car wrecks, I can work on contingency, and for criminal cases I get a flat fee up front.

"It's a good idea to think very carefully about a career in law before you set out. Most people have to borrow money to go to law school. Also, I would suggest getting a job in a law firm before making the decision to go to law school. A lot of lawyers are very difficult to get along with and work for, and you need to be aware of all the stresses involved before you get into it.

"Becoming a lawyer is a big decision. I don't think anyone should jump into it thinking they're, one, automatically going to get a job, or two, going to make a lot of money."

John Wiorek—Law Clerk

John Wiorek graduated law school summa cum laude and was editor of the *Law Review*. He works for an appellate judge in the Third District Illinois Appellate Court.

"*Law Clerk* isn't a title I'm particularly fond of. It makes people think you work in a grocery store or something. If I could change the job title, I'd call it something along the lines of *research attorney*. Sometimes we're called *elbow clerks* because we work at the elbow of the judge.

"Duties will vary depending on the judge you work with. In my case, writing and research are my primary duties. Every month we have court call. We handle both civil and criminal appeals. They've been to trial and, for one reason or another, the attorneys don't like the results so they file an appeal. They submit written arguments—*briefs,* they're called—and we get copies of those arguments. In the month that the case is scheduled to go before the court, we're sent the briefs. We're also sent the record—that is, the transcripts and common law records of all the original court proceedings.

"In Illinois each appellate judge gets two law clerks, so usually the other clerk and I will split up the work. We know what cases are set for the particular month and we have all of these stacks of briefs to read. The three of us—myself, the other law clerk, and the judge—make notes on the briefs and arguments. This could take three or four days.

"Then we have a conference and go through each case and discuss it. We give the judge our ideas on how the case should turn out.

"At the same time, we begin to research the law regarding those cases. We might work up a rough draft of decisions and do bench memos for other cases—giving a brief synopsis of the arguments and the law and what our feelings are about what the decision should or shouldn't be.

"The judge will listen to the oral arguments and come back and tell us what was decided, whether the original judgment was affirmed or reversed, and he'll explain the reasons for how the court reached the decision. We will then write a draft of the order.

"Any stress on the job would be mostly self-imposed. There are no hard-and-fast deadlines, although you do have to produce a certain amount of work in a certain amount of time. No judge likes to get behind on the caseload.

"Sometimes the work can get a bit repetitious—the issues can recur and they can be boring. Sometimes you read a two-thousand-page transcript and you're sitting there for three days reading some psychiatrist giving you his opinion about someone's sanity and going through his results of his MMPI and different psychological tests. It can get tedious.

"I like most the low level of stress and that it is nine to five, which gives me the opportunity to do other things. I teach a night course in criminal law at Western Illinois, and I can handle things on the side for clients if I want to.

"Plus, there is a certain satisfaction when you're done with a case, especially if the judges decide to make it an opinion rather than an order, which means it will be published. You can see in the books that you made a small contribution to developing the law.

"I wouldn't mind staying in this work, but I'm also considering full-time teaching as well. I get quite a kick out of it.

"Right now I earn around $44,000. The position at the college would start at $36,000, which would be a bit of a step down, at least initially. Private practice would pay more, but money isn't the biggest thing. The most important thing is to have control of my lifestyle."

How John Wiorek Got Started

"My decision to go into law came primarily from finding out after graduating with a bachelor's in psychology that the options were fairly limited with that kind of degree. So I spent some time kicking around a little bit, trying to decide the best route to go—a Ph.D. in psychology or law school. Although I had no great burning desire to go into law, law school seemed like the best option, something I'd be good at—based on my LSAT results—and something I thought had a fairly good potential for a job.

"I got my B.S. from Western Illinois University in Macomb in 1978. I attended law school at Southern Illinois University in Carbondale and finished in 1988 with a J.D.

"When I first got out of law school, I worked as a staff attorney on the Fifth District Appellate Court in Mt. Vernon, Illinois. Then, after six months, I started clerking for Judge Chapman and I worked for him for around two years. I started in my current position with Judge Kent Slater in December of 1990.

"Most of the time law clerk positions are temporary; one or two years is the norm. It is seen more as a stepping-stone to something else rather than as a career in itself. In fact, the reason I no longer work for the first judge is that he basically said to me, okay your two years are up and it's time for you to move on to something else. He thought I should be doing something 'better' for my career. I chose to continue as a law clerk with another judge because I found that I liked this kind of work, that I was good at it, and that I was comfortable with it. I didn't want to work with a firm. There are so many horror stories. The eighty-hour weeks. The grind. It didn't appeal to me at all.

"My job is nine to five. I get a steady paycheck; I know how much it's going to be. I don't work weekends or nights, and the stress level is really low."

Expert Advice from John Wiorek

"There are certain qualifications you have to have. If you want to be a law clerk, you're going to have to finish in at least the top quarter or probably the top 10 percent of your class. They're going to want you to have those good grades or be on *Law Review*.

"Also, you have to be able to write and like to write. If it's a real chore for you, it won't be the right job for you. Your analytical skills have to be fairly high, too.

"I would advise anyone to go for being a law clerk for at least one to two years. If you're thinking about making it a career, there are a couple of things to keep in mind. You'll make less money than in a firm. Plus, the job security isn't there. You serve at the whim of the judge you work for. He could retire or quit or not get re-elected, and then you're out of a job.

"Another point is to make sure you take a job with a judge you like and get along with. You spend a lot of time working closely together, so that's important. I'm lucky. I have a good judge to work for."

The Training You'll Need

To practice law in the courts of any state or other jurisdiction, a person must be licensed, or admitted to its bar, under rules established by the jurisdiction's highest court. Nearly all require that applicants for admission to the bar pass a written bar examination. Most jurisdictions also require applicants to pass a separate written ethics examination. Lawyers who have been admitted to the bar in one jurisdiction occasionally may be admitted to the bar in another without taking an examination if they meet that jurisdiction's standards of good moral character and have a specified period of legal experience.

Federal courts and agencies set their own qualifications for those practicing before them.

To qualify for the bar examination in most states, an applicant must complete at least three years of college and graduate from a law school approved by the American Bar Association (ABA) or the proper state authorities. (ABA approval signifies that the law school, particularly its library and faculty, meets certain standards developed by the association to promote quality legal education.)

Seven states accept the study of law in a law office or in combination with study in a law school; only California accepts the study of law by correspondence as qualifying for taking the bar examination.

Several states require registration and approval of students by a state board of law examiners, either before they enter law school or during the early years of legal study.

The required college and law school education usually takes seven years of full-time study after high school: four years of undergraduate study followed by three years in law school. Although some law schools accept a very small number of students after three years of college, most require applicants to have a bachelor's degree. To meet the needs of students who can attend only part-time, a number of law schools have night or part-time divisions, which usually require four years of study.

Acceptance by most law schools depends on several factors: the applicant's ability to demonstrate an aptitude for the study of law, usually through good undergraduate grades; the Law School Admission Test (LSAT); the quality of the applicant's undergraduate school; any prior work experience; and sometimes a personal interview. However, law schools vary in the weight that they place on each of these factors.

All law schools approved by the American Bar Association require that applicants take the LSAT. Nearly all law schools require that applicants have certified transcripts sent to the Law School Data Assembly Service. This service then sends applicants' LSAT scores and their standardized records of college grades to the law schools of their choice. Both this service and the LSAT are administered by the Law School Admission Services.

Graduates receive the degree of bachelor of law (LL.B.) or juris doctor (J.D.). Advanced law degrees may be desirable for those planning to specialize, do research, or teach. Some law students pursue joint degree programs, which generally require an additional year. Joint degree programs are offered in a number of areas, including law and business administration and law and public administration.

Earnings for Lawyers

Contrary to the experience of John Grisham's hero in *The Firm*, annual salaries of beginning lawyers in private industry average about $36,600. But top graduates from the nation's best law schools can start in some cases at over $80,000 a year. In the federal government, annual starting salaries for attorneys in 1993 were between $27,800 and $33,600, depending upon academic and personal qualifications.

Factors affecting the salaries offered to new graduates include: academic record; type, size, and location of employer; and specialized educational background.

Salaries of experienced attorneys also vary widely according to the type, size, and location of the employer. The average salary of the most experienced lawyers in private industry in 1992 was over $134,000, but some senior lawyers who were partners in the nation's top law firms earned over $1 million annually.

General attorneys in the federal government averaged around $62,200 a year in 1993. Lawyers on salary receive increases as they assume greater responsibility. Lawyers starting their own practices may need to work part-time in other occupations during the first years to supplement their incomes, which usually grow as their practices develop. Lawyers who are partners in law firms generally earn more than those who practice alone.

CHAPTER THREE

Judges

J udges preside over trials or hearings and listen as attorneys
representing the parties present and argue their cases. They
rule on the admissibility of evidence and methods of
conducting testimony, and they settle disputes between the
opposing attorneys. They ensure that rules and procedures are
followed, and if unusual circumstances arise for which standard
procedures have not been established, judges direct how the
trial will proceed based on their knowledge of the law.

Judges often hold pretrial hearings for cases during which
they listen to allegations and, based on the evidence presented,
determine whether the cases have enough merit for a trial to be
held. In criminal cases, judges may decide that persons charged
with crimes should be held in jail pending their trial or may set
conditions for release through the trial. In civil cases, judges may
impose restrictions upon the parties until a trial is held.

When trials are held, juries are often selected to decide cases.
However, judges decide cases when the law does not require a
jury trial, or when the parties waive the right to a jury. Judges
instruct juries on applicable laws, direct them to deduce the
facts from the evidence presented, and hear their verdicts. In
many states, judges sentence those convicted in criminal cases.
They also award relief to litigants, including, where appropriate, compensation for damages in civil cases.

Judges also work outside the courtroom in chambers. In their
private offices, judges read documents on pleadings and motions, research legal issues, hold hearings with lawyers, write
opinions, and oversee court operations. Running a court is like

running a small business, and judges manage their courts' administrative and clerical staff, too.

Judges' duties vary according to the extent of their jurisdictions and powers. General trial court judges of the federal and state court systems have jurisdiction over any case in their systems. They generally try those civil cases that transcend the jurisdiction of lower courts and all cases involving felony offenses.

Federal and state appellate court judges, although few in number, have the power to overrule decisions made by trial court or administrative law judges if they determine that legal errors were made in a case or if legal precedent does not support the judgment of the lower court. They rule on fewer cases and rarely have direct contacts with the people involved.

The majority of state court judges preside in courts in which jurisdiction is limited by law to certain types of cases. Various titles are assigned to these judges, but among the most common are municipal court judge, county court judge, magistrate, or justice of the peace. Traffic violations, misdemeanors, small-claims cases, and pretrial hearings constitute the bulk of the work of these judges, but some states allow them to handle cases involving domestic relations, probate, contracts, and selected other areas of the law.

Administrative law judges, formerly called hearing officers, are employed by government agencies to rule on appeals of agency administrative decisions. They make decisions on a person's eligibility for various Social Security benefits or worker's compensation, protection of the environment, enforcement of health and safety regulations, employment discrimination, and compliance with economic regulatory requirements.

Many judges work a standard forty-hour week, but a third of all judges work over fifty hours per week. Some judges with limited jurisdiction are employed part-time and divide their time between their judicial responsibilities and other careers.

Judges held ninety thousand jobs in 1992. All worked for federal, state, or local governments, with about half holding positions in the federal government. The majority of the remainder were employed at the state level.

Training

Most judges, although not all, have been lawyers first. All federal judges and state trial and appellate court judges are required to be lawyers or learned in law. About forty states presently allow nonlawyers to hold limited jurisdiction judgeships, but opportunities are better with law experience.

Federal administrative law judges must be lawyers and pass a competitive examination administered by the U.S. Office of Personnel Management. Many state administrative law judges and other hearing officials are not required to be lawyers, but law degrees are preferred for most positions.

Federal judges are appointed for life by the president, with the consent of the Senate. Federal administrative law judges are appointed by the various federal agencies with virtually lifetime tenure. About half of all state judges are appointed, while the remainder are elected in partisan or nonpartisan state elections.

Most state and local judges serve fixed terms, which range from four or six years for most limited jurisdiction judgeships to as long as fourteen years for some appellate court judges. Judicial nominating commissions, composed of members of the bar and the public, are used to screen candidates for judgeships in many states, as well as for federal judgeships.

All states have some type of orientation for newly elected or appointed judges. Thirteen states also require judges to take continuing education courses while serving on the bench.

Job Outlook

The prestige associated with serving on the bench should ensure continued intense competition for openings. Employment of judges is expected to grow more slowly than the average for all occupations. Contradictory social forces affect the demand for judges. Pushing up demand are public concerns about crime, safety, and efficient administration of justice; on the other hand, tight public funding should slow job growth.

Most job openings will arise as judges retire. Traditionally, many judges have held their positions until late in life. Now, early retirement is becoming more common, creating more job openings; however, becoming a judge will still be difficult. Besides competing with other qualified people, judicial candidates must gain political support in order to be elected or appointed.

Salaries

Federal district court judges had salaries of $133,600 in 1995, as did judges in the Court of Federal Claims. Circuit court judges earned $141,700 a year. Federal judges with limited jurisdiction, such as magistrates and bankruptcy court judges, had salaries of $122,900 in 1995. Full-time federal administrative law judges had average salaries of $94,800 in 1995. The Chief Justice of the United States Supreme Court earned $171,500 in 1995, and the associate justices earned $164,100.

Annual salaries of associate justices of state supreme courts averaged $91,093 in 1995, according to a survey by the National Center for State Courts, and ranged from about $64,452 to $131,085.

Salaries of state intermediate appellate court judges averaged $91,093 in 1995 but ranged from $64,452 to $131,085. Salaries of state judges with limited jurisdiction varied widely; many salaries are set locally.

What It's Really Like

James Lanuti—Circuit Court Judge

James Lanuti earned his J.D. at Illinois Institute of Technology–Chicago Kent College of Law in 1977. He is now a judge in the circuit court of LaSalle County in Illinois.

"I hear civil cases. I have divorce cases on my docket, I have paternity cases, I have lawsuits, personal injury cases, contract disputes. The lawsuits range in size from $2,500 all the way up to million-dollar suits and also some probate matters, estates, will contests, that sort of thing.

"I've handled just about everything. When I first went on the bench I did a lot of divorces cases. Then I spent four years doing traffic court where I heard the traffic cases as well as all the drunk driving cases, the serious traffic cases as well as reckless homicide cases, where people have been killed in drunk driving accidents, and some felonies—people charged with more serious crimes.

"At the same time I also heard the cases that are the most distressing—juvenile cases. I was the presiding judge of the juvenile court where I heard all the juvenile delinquency cases as well as cases involving abused and neglected children. I did that for about four years. Then I came back and did another stretch of civil cases. I was also in charge of probate cases for a while.

"In 1992 I was assigned to go to criminal court, and I spent about three and a half years there. I just came to civil court about a month ago—at my request. I was ready for a little change. I heard only murder cases, armed robbery, and so forth. It would be ideal to get a variety of criminal and civil cases, but in my county we separate the two.

"My caseload varies from day to day. If everything were litigated, you couldn't hear more than one case in a day. In an average day you might have thirty cases on your docket, but they all go away because they get settled. On another day you might only have half a dozen on the docket, but that might be a day you're in court all day because most of the cases are contested.

"We have juries come in on Mondays and we schedule all our jury trials on that day. If we need more time, we can do it on Tuesday and Wednesday. It doesn't usually take longer than a day to pick a jury, unless it's a big murder case. Then it can take more and we have to make special arrangements for that.

"A lot of times the only incentive to settle is that the case is going to be called to court. It's almost brinkmanship in negotiating some of these cases. The jury has to be there and ready to go before the parties will settle.

"The rest of the week we get more involved cases and we're very busy.

"I'm in here by eight or eight-thirty to get ready for the day. My first court call is at nine. If the cases resolve themselves, I can sometimes finish in court at three, but if not I'll be here until five.

"When I finish court early, I can use the time in chambers to familiarize myself with the next day's call. When I was a lawyer, I always appreciated a judge who took the time be prepared, to read the papers that the lawyers had filed. That isn't always the case, but that's one thing as a judge I've always shot for and to do it requires a certain amount of homework. You have to read the files, read the motions and the answers, and do some research.

"We don't have interns or law clerks but we do have a circuit clerk who is basically the record keeper and does the scheduling, like a clerk of the court. We do our own research.

"Obviously, the work is very interesting. It's not boring at all, and you see a lot of situations where you think you can make a difference. You can't always make everyone happy, though. Your first and foremost job is to follow the law. Sometimes that's not popular, but as long as you can do it consistently it will give you a sense of satisfaction. You're doing your part to administer justice.

"It can be frustrating sometimes if you end up having to hear cases that really should have been resolved before they came to court. You see a lot of people who are almost self-destructive. I see that a lot in divorce cases, like the movie *War of the Roses*. That's not totally untrue. And the saddest thing about it is to see the effect it has on children. That's one of the things we've tried to focus on in recent years in the court system on a national level. What can the courts do to make sure the children don't get lost in the shuffle? You have to realize, though, that the litigants have ultimate control over their own lives. You can't solve all of society's social problems. Even though you'd like to be able to get people to listen, sometimes they won't take your advice.

"It's also frustrating to see a juvenile come in, charged with a crime. You try to work with him—you talk to him, maybe give him probation and all sorts of other services. It's sad to see him come back a couple of years later charged with a felony as an adult who's going to go to prison.

"Once in a while you might worry about a decision on a tough case, but not often. I've felt comfortable with most of the decisions I've made. You have to have the ability to put the case behind you or else you won't be effective."

How James Lanuti Got Started

"I got my B.S. in math at the University of Illinois in 1969 and then worked as a computer program systems analyst for seven years. In fact, I worked while I went to law school at night. My goal at the time was to be able to work for myself and be independent, and I saw the law as a way to do that. I never intended at the time I started law school to become a judge. That was never a goal.

"I worked for a firm in Chicago for a couple of years and then I came to Ottawa because I had relatives in this area. My uncle is a lawyer here, and in 1979 I went to work with him.

"I also started working for the state attorney's office as a part-time assistant state attorney. I handled civil matters and represented the county government in county cases at the same time I was practicing law privately.

"The way the system works in the state of Illinois is that we have two levels of trial judges: associate judges and circuit judges. The associate judges are appointed by the circuit judges for four-year terms. The circuit judges are elected for six-year terms. The circuit judges have to run for retention on a yes/no ballet every six years.

"In 1986 there was a judicial vacancy for an associate judge, and I talked about it with my family and thought, 'Why not give it a try? If I don't get it I won't look back and worry about it.' But I got appointed.

"Whenever there's a vacancy for an associate judge a notice is posted at the courthouse and any lawyer can apply. Then all the circuit judges meet and vote via secret ballot.

"I knew the circuit judges at that point. That's one of the strong points of the system. The same lawyers who apply appear in the courtroom in front of the same judges who vote, so the judges already have a pretty good idea of the capabilities of the lawyers."

Advice from Judge Lanuti

"I don't think you start off considering a career as a judge. First, you decide if you want to get into the law, and if you want to be a lawyer, that's a career you choose. Once you're practicing law you'd know more about judges and know whether that's what you'd want to do.

"Some people are designed to be advocates—they can advocate a position strongly, even though the position might not be a good one. They don't judge their own clients. The client comes in and says, 'This is the position I want to take in this case' and the lawyer says, 'It's not unreasonable, so let's go ahead with it.' Other lawyers, though, might be more judgmental. They might say, 'Come on, Mr. Client, we'll never sell this to the jury. Let's compromise.' You see the practical route and the outcome and you're not wearing blinders just to advocate your client's position. If that's the way you operate, it might be an indication that you're better off being a judge.

"Being a judge has its advantages and disadvantages over being a lawyer. The advantage is that it is a somewhat prestigious position and you have respect in the community. Lawyers are often the victims of jokes but judges are highly respected. It's amazing to me how a lawyer becomes extremely wise once he or she becomes a judge.

"It's a steady position. You'll make a good living and you have a certain amount of freedom in the job. You're in charge of your docket and you're the one making the decisions. You can have some control with what's going on in front of you with the lawyers, and you get the holidays and the weekends off.

"But the idea of being your own boss is something you have to give up when you're a judge because now you're a public servant. You're no longer working for yourself; you're working for the public, and you have an obligation to be at work and be on the job.

"And though you do make a good living, you are giving up the opportunity to make substantially more as a lawyer. There are lawyers, obviously, who don't make as much money as judges, but there are many lawyers who make a lot more."

CHAPTER FOUR

Court Staff

B esides the obvious personnel you see buzzing around the courtroom—the lawyers and their staff and the judges— there are other key personnel who keep a courtroom running smoothly. Among these are court clerks, court reporters, and bailiffs.

Clerks of the Court

Court clerks administer the day-to-day dealings in courts of law. They oversee a staff of legal and administrative personnel who perform a variety of duties, such as preparing dockets of cases to be called; securing information for judges; and contacting witnesses, attorneys, and litigants to obtain information for court. Depending on the state and the level of the court, some clerks of the court may be elected; others may be appointed.

Training for Clerks of the Court

Although being an attorney is not a requirement for a clerk of the court position, more and more judges are preferring to work with experienced clerks who have more than administrative skills. The trend is for attorneys to be offered the position above other applicants. Educational requirements for attorneys are covered in Chapter 2.

Job Outlook for Clerks of the Court

As more and more courts are established to handle the increase in cases, more positions for clerks of the court will be opening. However, competition is keen and will continue to be so through the year 2005. Openings will occur primarily to replace existing workers who retire.

Salaries for Clerks of the Court

Salaries vary widely—from $40,000 to $80,000 per year—depending upon the region of the country and the level of the court.

Court Reporters

Written accounts of spoken words are necessary for records and legal proof. These verbatim reports of legal proceedings or other events are taken by court reporters.

Court reporters record all statements made in an official proceeding, often using stenotype machines. They take down all statements at speeds of approximately two hundred words per minute and present their records as the official transcripts. Because there is only one person creating an official transcript, accuracy is vitally important.

Many reporters do freelance work recording out-of-court depositions for attorneys, proceedings of meetings and conventions, and other private activities. Still others record the proceedings in the U.S. Congress, in state and local governing bodies, and in government agencies at all levels.

Some reporters still dictate notes on magnetic tapes that a typist can later transcribe. Others transcribe their own notes or give them to note readers, persons skilled in reading back shorthand notes.

Most commonly, reporters use stenotype machines that print shorthand symbols on paper and record them on computer disks. The disks are then loaded into a computer that translates and displays the symbols in English. This is called *computer-aided transcription*. Stenotype machines that link directly to the computer are used for real-time captioning. That is, as the reporter types the symbols, they are instantly transcribed by the computer. This is used for closed captioning for the deaf or hearing-impaired on television, in courts, or in meetings. Court reporters who specialize in captioning television news stories may be called *stenocaptioners*.

Court reporters can work a standard forty-hour week. Many court reporters, however, are self-employed and freelance their services, which may result in irregular hours. Others work part-time or as temporaries.

Although the work is not physically demanding, sitting in the same position for long periods can be tiring. In addition, pressure to be accurate and fast can be stressful.

Court reporters held 115,000 jobs in 1992. Nearly 15 percent were self-employed freelance court reporters. Of those who worked for a wage or salary, about one-third worked for state and local governments, a reflection of the large number of court reporters working in courts, legislatures, and various agencies.

Other court reporters worked for colleges and universities, secretarial and court reporting services, temporary help supply services, and law firms.

Training for Court Reporters

There are 350 postsecondary schools and colleges that offer two- or four-year training programs in court reporting. About 100 programs have been approved by the National Court Reporters Association, and all of them teach computer-aided transcription.

For court reporter jobs, employers prefer stenotype, not only because reporters can write faster using stenotype, but also because they can feed stenotype notes to a computer for high-speed transcription. Speed and accuracy are the most important factors in hiring. Court reporters in the federal government generally must take at least 175 words a minute, and many court reporting jobs require at least 225 words of dictation per minute.

Some states require court reporters who stenotype depositions to be notary publics, and eighteen states require each court reporter to be a Certified Court Reporter (CCR). A certification test is administered by a board of examiners in each state that has CCR laws.

The National Court Reporters Association confers the designation Registered Professional Reporter (RPR) upon those who pass a two-part examination and participate in continuing education programs. Although voluntary, the RPR designation is recognized as a mark of distinction in the profession.

Court reporters have little advancement opportunities, although some reporters choose to specialize in captioning television programs.

Job Outlook for Court Reporters

Employment of court reporters is expected to decline. Budget constraints should limit the ability of federal, state, and local courts to expand, even in the face of rising numbers of criminal court cases and civil lawsuits. Despite the decline, job openings will arise each year due to the need to replace workers who leave the occupation.

Demand should grow, however, for court reporters willing to take depositions for court reporting service bureaus or as independent freelancers. Another factor stimulating demand is the growing number of conventions, conferences, seminars, and similar meetings whose proceedings are recorded. Although many of these events are being videotaped, a written transcript must still be created for legal purposes or if the proceedings are to be published. The trend to provide instantaneous written captions for the deaf and hearing impaired also should strengthen demand for stenocaptioners.

Competition for entry-level jobs as a court reporter is increasing as more workers are attracted to the occupation. Opportunities should be best for those who earn certification by the National Court Reporters Association.

Salaries for Court Reporters

Court reporters had median earnings of $399 a week in 1994. The middle 50 percent earned between $306 and $629 a week. The lowest-paid 10 percent earned less than $232, while the highest-paid 10 percent earned over $790 a week. Court reporters generally earn higher salaries than stenographic office workers. Regardless of specialty, earnings depend on speed, education, experience, and geographic location (earnings are generally higher in large cities than in rural areas).

Bailiffs

Bailiffs are responsible for keeping order in the courtroom. They are also responsible for taking custody of the prisoners who are on trial and escorting them to and from holding cells.

Depending on the judge or the court system in which the bailiff works, he or she may have additional duties, including administrative tasks such as preparing the docket for the next day's cases, serving writs and subpoenas, and handling evictions or repossessions.

Job Outlook for Bailiffs

Employment of bailiffs is expected to increase more slowly than the average for all occupations through the year 2005. Employment growth will be tempered somewhat by continuing budgetary constraints faced by law enforcement agencies.

Although turnover in this and related law enforcement fields is among the lowest of all occupations, the need to replace workers who retire, transfer to other occupations, or stop working for other reasons will be the source of most job openings.

Training for Bailiffs

Qualifications expected for bailiffs will vary from jurisdiction to jurisdiction, but they are usually the same as for police officers. Candidates must have at least a high school education, a valid driver's license, and no criminal background.

Training often occurs on the job or in adjunct courses through the police academy. The training periods will also vary but can take from six months to a year.

Salaries for Bailiffs

Bailiffs and other law enforcement officers had a median annual salary of about $25,800 in 1994. The middle 50 percent earned between $20,500 and $30,900; the lowest-paid 10 percent were paid less than $15,600, while the highest-paid 10 percent earned over $38,800.

What It's Really Like

Gist Fleshman—Clerk of the Court

Gist Fleshman has a B.S. in political science from Illinois State University in Normal, Illinois. After working for a Congressman in Washington, D.C., for a couple of years, he went back to school and earned his J.D. from DePaul University in Chicago in 1985. He is clerk of the court for the Illinois Appellate Court Third District.

"My official job title is Clerk of the Appellate Court/Attorney. There are also clerks of the court who are not attorneys—it's a lower pay grade.

"The clerk of the court is the head administrative official in a court. He or she is the person who runs the court's operations on a day-to-day basis. The clerk may or may not answer to the judges, depending on the system.

"Here in Illinois we have at the trial level (circuit court) clerks of the court who are elected. In the appellate and state supreme court we have appointed clerks. People appeal to this court if they aren't happy with their trial results. This court reviews the original trial.

"What I do is about 40 percent legal, 60 percent administrative. I'm the day-to-day operations manager for the court. I deal with the public and press. I still handle all the motions that are filed in the court. The court has authorized me to make decisions on the routine ones. We get thousands of motions in, so the judge can authorize the staff to do it. The more complex issues I'll discuss with the motions judge, and maybe I'll even do research on them.

"As far as the administrative aspect, it's the usual. I make sure people show up and do their job. I make some policy decisions and take care of the maintenance of the building.

"I supervise eighteen people: staff attorneys, the chief deputy clerk and seven deputy clerks, and the maintenance and housekeeping staff. There are six judges in the court and each has two law clerks and one secretary.

"I get variety in my work without the stress. In the practice of law in a general firm you get the variety, too, but with a lot of stress to go along with it. I get to do legal work and I get to in some ways decide how much to do. If I don't have time I can delegate things to the research department. On the other hand, if it's something that's going to be a nice issue to get into and research—which is what I love to do—I can do it myself.

"At the same time I can negotiate with contractors and read blueprints, and study the contracts—that sort of thing. The courthouse is an historic building so there's always something to do there.

"The downsides are the same as for any administrator. It's the personnel problems. It's always uncomfortable and you have to deal with it and the thing I found is that subtle doesn't work. In my opinion, when a problem arises you take the person aside—you don't want to embarrass someone in front of other people—and you tell the person exactly what the problem is and exactly what you expect, and that usually takes care of it.

"But I enjoy working with people and the public. There's a lot of phone work, but I get to answer questions and help people.

"One of the things I love the most is that you can make a big difference. You definitely see injustices, where people have gotten a raw deal—people in prison who shouldn't be, or children who were taken away needlessly from their parents. Unlike in other jobs, here you can do something about it. You can pick up the phone and talk to a judge and tell him what's going on. You end up being a bit of an advocate for a party, but the judges listen to me. Wrongs can be righted. I love that aspect. It's very gratifying."

How Gist Fleshman Got Started

"I got my degree in political science. I enjoyed that but didn't want to do it for the rest of my life. I took some time off and realized I needed more than a political science degree and something that would allow me to go right away into a job. I considered an M.B.A. or a law degree, and the law degree sounded more interesting to me. But I'm not one of these people who knew from the time they were five they wanted to be a lawyer.

"Originally, I had planned to practice law, but I came here to this courthouse right out of law school as a staff attorney. There's a central research staff that functions the way law clerks do. I thought I'd stay one year, maybe two, then go out into private practice. After a year I went on a few interviews and was offered some jobs, but they really didn't interest me. I was really enjoying what I was doing so I thought I'd stay another year—and then another year went by. Then a couple of judges asked if I'd like to be their personal law clerk, which was a $7,000 a raise. I thought I'd do that for a year, then I'd definitely have to move on. But then, after a few months the research director, who is the day-to-day supervisor of the central staff attorneys, resigned and I was offered that position.

"I did that for two and a half years. At that time I was back in school taking more chemistry courses, thinking I might go into patent law. One reason for that was practicality. The market was starting to get glutted and that is one specialty today where there are a lot of openings. I kept thinking I'd move on and was preparing for that. When the clerk of the court started talking about retirement, I put in my name among the applicants and I was chosen. That was in 1992.

"I started out earning $21,500, and after each promotion I had a raise in salary. My pay went to $26,800 then jumped to $33,800, then I got raised to $41,000 when I became research director. Now I earn $61,500, and as far as I can tell, I'm one of the lowest-paid clerks in the country at the appellate court level.

"I've been here ten years—longer than any judge that's been here. That was one nice thing about going up through the ranks. The judges put a lot more trust in me than they would in someone they just hired from outside."

Expert Advice from Gist Fleshman

"You need to work your way up. The courts want someone with experience. Coming in as a staff attorney or law clerk is how to do it because you learn how the court works.

"And in some ways it's a position you can create for yourself because it's something that's developing. If you prove yourself and put a bug in the judge's ear, you could make the job be what you want it to be.

"But it's very competitive and you need to make sure you have excellent reading and writing skills."

Dan P. Clark—Court Reporter

Dan Clark is a court reporter and partner in Maffei & Clark Court Reporting Service in San Rafael, California. He has been working in the field since 1976.

"Maffei & Clark Court Reporting Service supplies court reporting services for the legal industry. The major thrust of our service revolves around reporting depositions; however, we also report arbitrations, examinations under oath. We have five reporters we work with. All of our reporters are on an independent-contractor basis and are not employees.

"I enjoy my job—some days. It's important to remember that a deposition is usually an adversarial proceeding. Personalities can get very intense. A typical day would be for me to go to my deposition, never in the same location. I swear the witness in and take a verbatim record of what's said. I usually find my job interesting, as I get to go different places and meet different people every day, but occasionally I get a little bored, especially with contract law cases. Sometimes it's very, very busy and all the clients wants their transcripts yesterday, and then sometimes, it's slow. Depositions go on and off at the drop of the hat, so you have no idea really what days you'll actually end up working or where.

"I think the only thing that really bothers me are people who are not concerned what kind of a record they are making. But I do get to meet a variety of people. I learn something at every deposition I take. I take depositions from people in every walk of life, from a neurosurgeon to a baker to an industrial engineer."

How Dan Clark Got Started

"I had two years of college then attended a court reporting school in Denver, Colorado, for two and a half years. I'm a Certified Shorthand Reporter (CSR), which is the state certification. I'm also a Registered Professional Reporter (RPR), which is the national certification.

"I was working as a court clerk in Denver County Court and knew I needed to get schooling in something. I was a fairly fast typist. An attorney noticed how fast I could type and said, 'Hey, you should go to court reporting school.' My response was, 'That's exactly what I've been looking for!'

"After school was over in Denver, I moved to San Francisco. I had a friend who worked as an office manager for a court reporting firm. I sat in on a deposition, and they hired me on the spot. I worked for them for seven years, then became a partner. I then left and formed my own company. For the last eight years, I've had a partnership."

Expert Advice from Dan Clark

"Make sure you have a good background in English. You should have a curiosity about life. You should be able to concentrate. You also need good computer skills.

"Becoming a Certified Shorthand Reporter is very difficult to do. People watch us and think, 'Oh, that looks easy. They're hardly moving.' But that's not the case.

"When you go to school, don't give up. Only one-third of the people who enter court reporting school actually get out of school and become certified. Many people don't realize how very difficult it is. For example, in order to become certified in California, you must be able to write four voice testimonies at 225 words a minute. That's a real challenge!"

Kent Reeves—Deputy Bailiff

Kent Reeves is a deputy bailiff with the Fairborn/Beavercreek Municipal Court in Fairborn, Ohio. He has two associate's degrees and a bachelor's degree in American jurisprudence from Wright State University in Dayton, Ohio. He began his current job in 1985.

"I have an extremely busy job. I work anywhere from forty to fifty hours a week. Right now we have a chief bailiff and two deputies. Our caseload has increased so much that there is talk of having a third deputy, a security officer, and a secretary.

"I take care of court security and other administrative tasks in the court. I am responsible for the safety of the judge and magistrate. I take control over people the judge sentences in court and I place them in a holding cell to be turned over to the police or a jailer. And when prisoners come to court from the jail, I am responsible for them as well.

"On the administrative end, I prepare cases for the next day's docket and make sure all the paperwork is available for the judge. When we call the cases in the courtroom, the judge does not have to go searching through the jackets to find information. We also print out the official docket from the computer and match that with the cases we have. Our office prides itself on having the information even before the judge wants it.

"I also serve subpoenas, writs, notices, and summonses for both the criminal docket and civil or small-claims court. And I evict tenants and take back real property, such as repossessing cars. Repossession can be handled by a finance company;

however, if a plaintiff in a civil case gets a monetary judgment, we can take personal property to satisfy the judgment. Also a plaintiff, such as a car lot or a furniture company, might ask the court for return of a specific property such as a car or stereo set.

"Most of the time my job is not too dangerous; however, it does have its moments. Every now and then, we must chase after escaped prisoners or try to serve someone or obtain real property from someone who does not want to be cooperative.

"We wear suit and ties in the court. After hours we can wear anything. A lot of times I come home to change into jeans and a T-shirt when I go out to serve papers. It's more comfortable and also a lot of people will be more responsive than if they see a 'suit' coming up their walk.

"Salaries for Fairborn bailiffs run between $30,000 and $40,000 a year. I am an employee of the court; however, our pay and benefits come from the city of Fairborn. Sometimes the workload is so heavy that my salary seems to work out to below minimum wage. However, compared to what other bailiffs make in our area, I do very well.

"The work atmosphere is extremely busy, not just for me but the court as a whole. We are one of the busiest, single-judge courts in the state, according to the supreme court report.

"I think my favorite part of my job is the interaction that I have with a variety of people. I try to treat people the way I would want to be treated if our roles were reversed. By doing this, most everyone responds positively. And even when I have to lock people up, they usually don't give me any problems.

"The thing I dislike most is that being around a certain element of society all day sometimes makes me cynical and distrustful."

How Kent Reeves Got Started

"When I was around eighteen I wanted to be a lawyer. That changed after I finished my bachelor's degree. I came to the conclusion that I could not defend the ones I thought were guilty, nor could I prosecute those I thought were innocent.

"I studied for two associates degrees—one in law enforcement and one in medical lab technology. I did this to help get a job either as a police officer or forensic investigator. Also, I planned to use the B.A., if I had the opportunity, to obtain a federal law enforcement position.

"I was looking for a job as a forensic investigator when I heard of an opening in the adult probation office as a probation officer in common pleas, the court that handles the felonies and domestic relations cases—divorce and probate, for example. They passed my name on to Fairborn's municipal court probation office. Although I did not get the job, the clerk of the court called back about three weeks later to ask if I would like the position of bailiff.

"I was disappointed at first, but now I'm glad that I'm a bailiff instead of a probation officer. As a bailiff, you are sometimes the judge's ambassador to the community. You have more of a chance to meet both sides.

"I started in 1985, and my training was on the job at the time. The most important rule they teach us is politeness. Always remember, the roles could be reversed. Training also focused on the laws covering bailiffs, requirements for serving papers, and other bailiff functions.

"When I was hired, there was no standardized training for bailiffs. Training was done on the job. This is true of practically all bailiffs in the state. My training period lasted about six months. Two years after I was hired, the state of Ohio began to try to organize some sort of standardization for the roles of bailiffs and began to enact laws concerning them. That helped establish the Basic Bailiffs Training course at the Ohio Peace Officers Academy in London, Ohio. When the program was set up, I was sent to it for additional training."

Sound Advice from Kent Reeves

"Don't do this job if you are thin-skinned or don't want to work hard. Long hours are not uncommon. If you think that a bailiff job is nine to five, then you should look elsewhere.

"Although most people think that the courts are an arm of the police, we are really the arena that both sides use. A lot of times you get just as much abuse from the police as you do from the defendants. Since we are usually the contact between the police and the courts, when something happens that the police don't like, they usually vent their frustrations on the bailiffs. Also, as bailiffs we are in charge of court security—which sometimes they can't understand. We must take it in stride.

"To prepare yourself when you start out job hunting to be a bailiff, I would suggest classes that would help you understand the legal system in your state and/or community. Bailiffs in jurisdictions our size or smaller are usually hired by the judge. In larger jurisdictions, they are probably hired by the chief bailiff or the clerk of the court, so that's the best place to see about openings."

CHAPTER FIVE

Paralegals

P aralegals work directly under the supervision of lawyers, who often delegate to paralegals many of the tasks they perform as lawyers. The lawyers assume responsibility for the legal work; paralegals are prohibited from setting legal fees, giving legal advice, or presenting a case in court.

Paralegals generally do background work for lawyers. To help prepare cases for trial, paralegals investigate the facts of cases to make sure that all relevant information is uncovered. Paralegals may conduct legal research to identify the appropriate laws, judicial decisions, legal articles, and other materials that may be relevant to clients' cases. After organizing and analyzing all the information, paralegals may prepare written reports that attorneys use to decide how cases should be handled.

Should attorneys decide to file lawsuits on behalf of clients, paralegals may help prepare the legal arguments, draft pleadings to be filed with the court, obtain affidavits, and assist the attorneys during trials. Paralegals also keep files of all documents and correspondence important to cases.

Besides litigation, paralegals may also work in areas such as bankruptcy, corporate, criminal, employee benefits, patent and copyright, and real estate law. They help draft documents such as contracts, mortgages, separation agreements, and trust instruments. They may help prepare tax returns and plan estates. Some paralegals coordinate the activities of the other law office employees and keep the financial records for the office.

Paralegals who work for corporations help attorneys with such matters as employee contracts, shareholder agreements, stock option plans, and employee benefit plans. They may help prepare and file annual financial reports, maintain corporate minutes books and resolutions, and help secure loans for the corporation. Paralegals may also review government regulations to make sure that the corporation operates within the law.

The duties of paralegals who work in government vary depending on the type of agency that employs them. Generally, paralegals in government analyze legal material for internal use, maintain reference files, conduct research for attorneys, collect and analyze evidence for agency hearings, and prepare informative or explanatory material on the law, agency regulations, and agency policy for general use by the agency and the public.

Paralegals employed in community legal service projects help the poor, the aged, and other persons in need of legal aid. They file forms, conduct research, and prepare documents. When authorized by law, they may represent clients at administrative hearings.

Some paralegals, usually those in small and medium-sized law firms, have varied duties. One day the paralegal may do research on judicial decisions on improper police arrests and the next day may help prepare a mortgage contract. This requires a general knowledge of many areas of the law.

Some paralegals who work for large law firms, government agencies, and corporations specialize in one area of the law. Some specialties are real estate, estate planning, family law, labor law, litigation, and corporate law. Even within specialties, functions often are broken down further so that paralegals may deal with one narrow area within the specialty. For example, paralegals who specialize in labor law may deal exclusively with employee benefits.

A growing number of paralegals are using computers in their work. Computer software packages are increasingly used to search legal literature stored in the computer and identify legal texts relevant to a specific subject. In litigation that involves many supporting documents, paralegals may use computers to organize and index the material. Paralegals may also use computer software packages to perform tax computations and explore the consequences of possible tax strategies for clients.

Paralegals employed by corporations and government work a standard forty-hour week. Although most paralegals work year-round, some are temporarily employed during busy times of the year then released when work diminishes. Paralegals who work for law firms sometimes work very long hours when they are under pressure to meet deadlines. Some law firms reward such loyalty with bonuses and additional time off.

Paralegals handle many routine assignments, particularly when they are inexperienced. Some find that these assignments offer little challenge and become frustrated with their duties. However, paralegals usually assume more responsible and varied tasks as they gain experience. Furthermore, as new laws and judicial interpretations emerge, paralegals are exposed to many new legal problems that make their work more interesting and challenging.

In summary, the duties of a paralegal are as follows:

1. Takes direct responsibility from the attorney for a variety of functions, such as drafting motions, interrogatories to the opposing side, complaints, and correspondence.

2. Regularly deals directly with clients and opposing counsel.

3. At the discretion of the attorney, is autonomous in some areas and has authority when dealing with opposing counsel.

4. Does legal research.

5. Prepares flow charts in complex cases.

6. Prepares cases for trial, e.g., trial binders and evaluation of evidence.

In short, paralegals are used in ways that junior clerks or law clerks in very large firms were used fifty years ago. Such firms now hire more paralegals, or legal assistants, and fewer attorneys just out of law school. The paralegal's job has become more invoved with research at the discretion of the attorney.

Paralegals held about ninety-five thousand jobs in 1992. Private law firms employed the vast majority; most of the remainder worked for various levels of government. Paralegals are found in nearly every federal government agency; the General Services Administration and the Departments of Justice, Treasury, Interior, and Health and Human Services are the largest employers.

State and local governments and publicly funded legal service projects employ paralegals as well. Banks, real estate development companies, and insurance companies also employ small numbers of paralegals.

Training

There are several ways to enter the paralegal profession, but employers generally require formal paralegal training. Several types of training programs are acceptable; however, some employers prefer to train their paralegals on the job, promoting experienced legal secretaries or hiring persons with college education but no legal experience. Other entrants have experience in a technical field that is useful to law firms, such as a background in tax preparation for tax and estate practice or nursing or health administration for personal injury practice.

Over six hundred formal paralegal training programs are offered by four-year colleges and universities, law schools, community and junior colleges, business schools, and proprietary schools. In 1993, 177 programs had been approved by the American Bar Association (ABA). Although this approval is neither required nor sought by many programs, graduation from an ABA-approved program can enhance one's employment opportunities. The requirements for admission to formal training programs vary widely. Some require some college courses or a bachelor's degree. Others accept high school graduates or persons with legal experience. A few schools require standardized tests and personal interviews.

Most paralegal programs are completed in two years, although some take as long as four years and award a bachelor's degree upon completion. Other programs take only a few months to complete but require a bachelor's degree for admission.

Programs typically include a combination of general courses, on subjects such as the law and legal research techniques, and courses that cover specialized areas of the law, such as real estate, estate planning and probate, litigation, family law, contracts, and criminal law. Many employers prefer applicants with training in a specialized area of the law. Programs also increasingly include courses that introduce students to the legal applications of computers.

Many paralegal training programs include an internship in which students gain practical experience by working for several months in a law office, corporate legal department, or government agency. Experience gained in internships is an asset when seeking a job after graduation. Depending on the program, graduates may receive a certificate, an associate degree, or, in some cases, a bachelor's degree.

The quality of paralegal training programs varies; the better programs generally emphasize job placement. Prospective students should examine the experiences of recent graduates of programs in which they are considering enrolling.

Paralegals need not be certified, but the National Association of Legal Assistants has established standards for voluntary certification that require various combinations of education and experience. Paralegals who meet these standards are eligible to take a two-day examination given each year at several regional testing centers by the Certifying Board of Legal Assistants of the National Association of Legal Assistants. Those who pass this examination are designated Certified Legal Assistants (CLAs). This designation is a sign of competence in the field and may enhance employment and advancement opportunities.

Paralegals must be able to handle legal problems logically and effectively communicate, both orally and in writing, their findings and opinions to their supervising attorney. They must understand legal terminology and have good research and investigative skills. Familiarity with the operation and applications of computers in legal research and litigation support is increasingly important. Paralegals must always stay abreast of new developments in the law that affect their area of practice.

Because paralegals often deal with the public, they must be courteous and uphold the high ethical standards of the legal profession. A few states have established ethical guidelines that paralegals in the state must follow.

Experienced paralegals usually are given progressively more responsible duties and less supervision. In large law firms, corporate legal departments, and government agencies, experienced paralegals may supervise other paralegals and clerical staff and delegate work assigned by the attorneys. Advancement opportunities include promotion to managerial and other law-related positions within the firm or corporate legal department. However, some paralegals find it easier to move to another law firm when seeking increased responsibility or advancement.

Job Outlook

Employment of paralegals is expected to grow much faster than the average for all occupations through the year 2005. Job opportunities are expected to expand as more employers become aware that paralegals are able to do many legal tasks for lower salaries than lawyers. Both law firms and other employers with legal staffs should continue to emphasize hiring paralegals so that the cost, availability, and efficiency of legal services can be improved.

Rapid employment growth will create most of the job openings for paralegals in the future. Other job openings will arise as people leave the occupation. Although the number of job openings for paralegals is expected to increase significantly through the year 2005, so will the number of persons pursuing this career. Thus, keen competition for jobs should continue as the growing number of graduates from paralegal training programs keeps pace with employment growth. Still, job prospects are expected to be favorable for graduates of highly regarded formal programs.

Private law firms will continue to be the largest employers of paralegals as a growing population needs more legal services. The growth of prepaid legal plans also should contribute to the demand for the services of law firms. A growing array of other organizations, such as corporate legal departments, insurance companies, real estate and title insurance firms, and banks, will also hire paralegals.

Job opportunities for paralegals will expand even in the public sector. Community legal service programs that provide assistance to the poor, the aged, minorities, and middle-income families operate on limited budgets and will employ more paralegals to keep expenses down and serve the most people. Federal, state, and local government agencies, consumer organizations, and the courts also should continue to hire paralegals in increasing numbers.

To a limited extent, paralegal jobs are affected by the business cycle. During recessions, demand declines for some discretionary legal services, such as planning estates, drafting wills, and handling real estate transactions. Corporations are less inclined to initiate litigation when falling sales and profits lead to fiscal belt tightening. As a result, full-time paralegals employed in offices adversely affected by a recession may be laid off or have their work hours reduced.

On the other hand, during recessions, corporations and individuals are more likely to face other legal problems, such as bankruptcies, foreclosures, and divorces, that require legal assistance.

Furthermore, the continuous emergence of new laws and judicial interpretations of existing laws creates new business for lawyers and paralegals without regard to the business cycle.

Salaries

Earnings of paralegals vary greatly. Salaries depend on the education, training, and experience the paralegal brings to the job, the type and size of employer, and the geographic location of the job. Generally, paralegals who work for large law firms or in large metropolitan areas earn more than those who work for smaller firms or in less-populated regions.

Paralegals had an average annual salary of about $31,700 in 1993, according to a compensation survey by Kenneth Leventhal & Company for the National Federation of Paralegal Associations. Starting salaries of paralegals ranged from a low of $14,000 to a high of $32,000 a year, according to the same survey.

In addition to salary, many paralegals received an annual bonus, which averaged more than $1,600 in 1993. Employers of the majority of paralegals provided life and health insurance benefits and contributed to a retirement plan on their behalf.

Paralegal specialists hired by the federal government in 1994 started at $20,000 to $25,200 a year, depending on their training and experience. The average annual salary of paralegals who worked for the federal government in 1995 was about $39,800.

What It's Really Like

Barbara Grace Lake—Legal Assistant

Barbara Grace Lake recently retired after working in the field for twenty years. She worked for small plaintiff personal injury (P.I.) firms and large insurance defense firms.

"A typical day would begin by checking to see what things I had on the calendar for that day: interrogatories that needed to be answered, a complaint that needed to be filed within the next two weeks, whether we had received medical charts from a client's doctor so that my attorney could begin settlement negotiations, etc. If we were still waiting for interrogatory answers from a client, I might have needed to make phone calls to see what the hang-up was. I have even gone to clients' homes to get their answers to interrogatories. If it looked as if we were not going to make the deadline for answers, I'd need to call opposing counsel to arrange for an extension. If opposing counsel was late with his or her answers and had not requested an extension, I'd need to write rather than phone, explaining that he or she had now waived the right to object to any answers and that we expected full answers by a specific date. If I had calendared that such full answers were expected but not received, I'd prepare a motion to compel and file it with the court.

"Next, I'd check the mail. If our complaint had been answered, I would prepare and send interrogatories to opposing counsel for their client to answer. I would also notice their client's deposition and determine what documents we wanted for a request to produce. If opposing counsel filed a motion to compel answers to interrogatories, I would prepare the response to have filed in the court.

"On a monthly basis (two months in advance) I'd pull all cases that needed a complaint filed with the court. There is a one-year statute of limitations in personal injury cases, so if a person was injured on March 1, 1995, a complaint would have to be filed on or before March 1, 1996. Usually I would draft the complaint for the attorney to sign. In unusually complex cases, I would ask for the attorney's input as to any special clauses to be included. This is one of the few areas where a mistake can be deadly. If a complaint is not filed on time, our client has lost the right to sue, and the only remedy would be to sue the attorney for malpractice. Almost any other deadline can be negotiated, but not this one.

"If opposing counsel filed a motion against us, after checking with counsel as to general areas of defense, it would be my job to check legal citations for authorities to cover ourselves. That's the name of the game.

"The work is tense and intense. Every day brought a new set of deadlines. Every day was a juggling act. I'd be working on one document trying to get it out of the way so it could get down to court, but before I could finish that, another document had to be completed because the attorney signing it was leaving at 11:00 A.M. for a deposition and wouldn't be back in time for it to be signed and in today's mail. Then I'd hurry to finish the next because a client was coming in, and it just went on and on.

"A legal assistant hits the door at a run and, after working a ten- or eleven-hour day, doesn't stop running until he or she is in the car going home. Half the time I had to take work home to finish and bring in first thing in the morning. My average work week was fifty to seventy hours.

"Some of my work was really quite dull: research, deposition indices in cases going to trial, flow charts, and dramatis personae charts. But all of it was under time pressure. That's the nature of the business.

"On the plus side was the satisfaction in doing a difficult job ably and well. Also, from receptionists to attorneys, one's co-workers are generally brighter than the average found in, for instance, a large insurance office or state agency.

"By the same token, bright people under intense pressure can sometimes be downright churlish. The constant pressure, then, I believe, is a major drawback. Then, too, unless a legal assistant wants to go to law school, it's a dead-end job. Legal assistants are already at the top of their field and there is nowhere to go up."

How Barbara Lake Got Started

"Although I completed two years of undergraduate work, this did not occur until 1988 at American River College in Sacramento, California. Most legal assistants hired since 1985 must complete a college-level course preparing them for the field. In my case, I went to work in a very small plaintiff personal injury firm and was trained by the attorneys. I still maintain that the best training in the world for a legal assistant is to work for three lazy attorneys who are more than happy to let him or her do the work. I was hired because I was able to write.

"Just prior to looking for work in the legal field I was a senior clerk in charge of a branch office of Department of Rehabilitation in Reseda, California. I was called for jury duty. I was so intrigued by the workings of the law during jury duty—by the attorneys each playing their hands to their client's best advantage, by the judge—that I felt I had to get into this field of work."

Advice from Barbara Lake

"By all means take whatever courses are offered in your area to help prepare you for the job ahead. Always be scrupulously honest. By that I mean direct. If an attorney asks if you if you know something and you don't, don't hedge. Answer honestly, 'I do not know, but give me ten minutes and I'll have an answer for you,' and then get that answer.

"Join whatever legal assistant or paralegal organization is in your area and develop contacts in other law offices. As long as you are not working at opposite ends of a court case, some of your best help is going to come from more experienced legal assistants. Don't try to go it alone. All you will get for your pains is an ulcer."

CHAPTER SIX

Legal Secretaries

*L*egal secretaries are responsible for a variety of administrative and clerical duties that are necessary to run and maintain organizations efficiently. They schedule appointments, give information to callers, organize and maintain files, fill out forms, and take dictation. They may also type letters, make travel arrangements, or contact clients. In addition, secretaries operate office equipment such as facsimile machines, photocopiers, and telephones with voice mail capabilities.

More specifically, the duties of a legal secretary generally include the following:

1. Prepares (with a typewriter or computer) documents, correspondence, pleadings, etc., at the direction of the legal assistant/paralegal or attorney.

2. Is knowledgeable about court filing rules and fees and is responsible to see to it that documents are properly filed.

3. Keeps legal calendar for attorneys.

4. Proofreads documents for factual, grammatical, or typographical errors.

5. Maintains files in good order.

6. Handles phones.

The legal secretary's job in most large firms, then, is one of production at the direction of attorneys and legal assistants. Except in matters of obvious routine and the use of company formats, the legal secretary does not independently generate work. In some small firms, though, jobs and job titles are often blurred, with the assistant or paralegal on occasion doing the work of a secretary and the secretary at times doing the work of an assistant. (For more information on paralegals or legal assistants, see Chapter 5.)

In today's automated offices, secretaries increasingly use personal computers to run spreadsheet, word processing, database management, desktop publishing, and graphics programs for tasks previously handled by managers and professionals. Because they are often relieved from dictation and typing, legal secretaries can support several members of the professional staff. Secretaries sometimes work in clusters of three or four so that they can work more flexibly and share their expertise.

In addition to general administrative duties, further specialization in various types of law is common among legal secretaries. They prepare correspondence and legal papers such as summonses, complaints, motions, and subpoenas under the supervision of an attorney. They also may review legal journals and assist in other ways with legal research.

Secretaries generally work a standard forty-hour week. In some cities, especially in the Northeast, the scheduled work-week is thirty-seven hours or less.

Secretaries held more than 3.3 million jobs in 1994, making this one of the largest occupations in the U.S. economy. The following tabulation shows the distribution of employment by secretarial specialty:

Legal secretaries	281,000
Medical secretaries	226,000
All other secretaries	2,842,000

About one-half of all secretaries are employed in firms providing services, ranging from education and health to legal and business services.

Training

High school graduates may qualify for secretarial positions provided they have basic office skills. Today, however, knowledge of word processing, spreadsheet, and database management programs is increasingly important, and most employers require it. Secretaries must be proficient in keyboarding and good at spelling, punctuation, grammar, and oral communication. Shorthand is necessary for some positions.

Employers also look for communication and interpersonal skills, since secretaries must be tactful in their dealings with many different people. Discretion, judgment, organizational ability, and initiative are important for higher-level secretarial positions.

As office automation continues to evolve, retraining and continuing education will remain an integral part of many jobs. Continuing changes in the office environment, for instance, have increased the demand for secretaries who are adaptable and versatile. Secretaries may have to attend classes to learn to operate new office equipment such as word processing equipment, information storage systems, personal computers, or new and updated software packages.

The skills needed for a secretarial job can be acquired in various ways. Formal training, especially for computer skills, may lead to higher-paying jobs. Secretarial training ranges from high school vocational education programs that teach office practices, shorthand, and keyboarding skills to one- or two-year programs in secretarial science offered by business schools, vocational-technical institutes, and community colleges. Many temporary service agencies provide training in computer and keyboarding skills. Training in specific software programs is often acquired, however, through instruction offered at the workplace by other employees or by equipment and software vendors. In addition, specialized training programs are available for students planning to become legal secretaries.

Testing and certification for entry-level office skills are available through the Office Proficiency Assessment and Certification (OPAC) program offered by Professional Secretaries International (PSI). As secretaries gain experience, they can earn the designation of Certified Professional Secretary (CPS) by passing a series of examinations given by the Institute for Certifying Secretaries, a department of PSI. This designation is recognized by a growing number of employers as the mark of excellence for senior-level office professionals.

Similarly, those without experience who want to be certified as a legal support professional may be certified as an Accredited Legal Secretary (ALS) by the certifying board of the National Association of Legal Secretaries. This organization also administers an examination to certify legal secretaries with three years of experience as Professional Legal Secretaries (PLSs).

Job Outlook

Employment of secretaries is expected to grow more slowly than the average for all occupations through the year 2005. Nevertheless, employment opportunities should be quite plentiful, especially for well-qualified and experienced secretaries, who, according to many employers, are in short supply. The very large size of the field, coupled with moderate turnover, generates several hundred thousand secretarial positions each year as experienced workers transfer to other occupations or leave the labor force.

Demand for secretaries will rise as the economy grows and as more workers are employed in offices. The trend toward secretaries assuming more responsibilities traditionally reserved for managers and professionals should also stimulate demand.

Increased productivity resulting from new office technologies, however, will offset this demand somewhat. In firms that have invested in electronic typewriters, word processors, or personal computers, secretaries can turn out significantly more work than when they used electric or manual typewriters. New office technologies such as electronic mail, facsimile machines, and voice message systems are used in a growing number of organizations. These and other sophisticated computer software capabilities are expected to be used more widely in the years ahead.

Widespread use of automated equipment is already changing the work flow in many offices. Administrative duties are being reassigned and the functions of entire departments are being restructured. Large firms are experimenting with different methods of staffing their administrative support operations. In some cases, such traditional secretarial duties as typing or keyboarding, filing, copying, and accounting are being assigned to workers in other units or departments.

In some law offices paralegals are taking over some tasks formerly done by secretaries. Professionals and managers increasingly do their own word processing rather than submit the work to secretaries and other support staff. In addition, there is a trend in many offices for groups of professionals and managers to share secretaries, allowing secretaries to assume new responsibilities.

Developments in office technology are certain to continue, and they will bring about further changes in the secretary's work environment. However, many secretarial job duties are of a personal, interactive nature and hence not easily automated. Duties such as planning schedules, receiving clients, and transmitting staff instructions require tact and communication skills. Because automated equipment cannot substitute for these personal skills, secretaries will continue to play a key role in the office activities of most organizations.

Salaries

The average annual income for all legal secretaries was $26,700 in 1993. Salaries vary a great deal, however, reflecting differences in skill, experience, and level of responsibility, ranging from $19,100 to $38,400.

The starting salary for inexperienced secretaries in the federal government was $16,700 a year in 1995. All secretaries employed by the federal government in 1995 averaged about $25,800.

What It's Really Like

Jennifer Franks—Legal Secretary

Jennifer Franks is a legal secretary and an assistant estate administrator in a general-practice law firm specializing in family law, estate planing, estate administration, real estate transactions, and assorted other areas. She works in Delaware County, Pennsylvania.

"The firm I work for is a very old, well-established firm on the Main Line in Delaware County, Pennsylvania. We have only five attorneys, but we have quite a history.

"My days usually consist of translating dictation into letters to clients and other attorneys or judges or whomever. Unfortunately, there are often some personal items that come into play, but I suppose the bosses feel that as long as I'm typing I can type a personal letter for them, too. It's not always appreciated by me, though.

"I would normally handle the attorney's incoming mail except that he really likes to open it himself. The only bad thing about this is that it doesn't get date-stamped, so later on it's hard to tell when things came into the office, which can be important.

"I'm not supposed to have to answer the phones, but I often do because our receptionist sometimes needs a break. Most of the phone calls go straight to the attorney unless he's on the phone, in which case they are often transferred to me. I find out if I can answer a question or be of any assistance or just take a message. Oftentimes the caller just needs some information that I can retrieve from a file and pass along, but knowing what's confidential and what isn't is important. If I have any doubts, I let the attorney handle it. So far, I've been lucky.

"I also make appointments for the attorney I work for, although, again, he likes to handle this kind of thing himself.

"I work from nine to five every day and have an hour for lunch. Our workplace is full of camaraderie and laughter. It's like a second family. Sometimes we have fights and get on each other's nerves, but for the most part we know that we rely heavily on each other for mutual support.

"It's a really good feeling to know that the attorneys feel you are competent and that they appreciate your hard work. Being an assistant is extremely rewarding even if you're not making all the decisions.

"I suppose the part I like least about my job is stigma that is attached to it. People seem to think that because you're a secretary you can't do anything else. (Just wait until they need one!) As far as the actual daily work goes, the least favorite part of the job is having to be at the beck and call of someone else. You report to people higher up, and they have control of what you do with your time. Sometimes I wish that I were the one making all the decisions about the cases that I see because sometimes I don't always agree with the decisions the attorneys make. But that's not up to me. I didn't go to law school so I can't say that what the attorney is advising is totally wrong. But I think it's appropriate to voice your opinion sometimes. On a few occasions I have asked my boss why he made the decision he did; could he enlighten me to how he came to that end. Sometimes clarification is all I really need. Luckily he understands that I'm just paying attention and that I don't mean to doubt him, I'm just curious. I think any smart, well-adjusted attorney can appreciate an inquisitive mind."

How Jennifer Franks Got Started

"I received a bachelor's in elementary education from a well-known university in Philadelphia in 1991. I became a legal secretary because the job was offered to me by my best friend's mother, who had her own two-person practice. I took the job in September of 1991 because, at the time, I was fairly certain that after all the years of college for a degree in elementary education, I really didn't want to teach—not yet, anyway. I had never worked as a legal secretary before and had no idea what I was doing. My friend had been the secretary there for some time, but she had been offered a job in her field as a civil engineer.

"She showed me around the office on a Saturday afternoon, using words I had never heard before, such as 'pleadings.' I was swimming in fear that I would botch everything. I had never even used the word processing program before. Every last detail was new to me. The only thing I had going for me was that I knew I was capable of doing the job, and I knew that Amy's mother liked me. Other than that I was lost.

"But within about two weeks I had it down pat. I knew the lingo and the word processing program. I was also really enjoying the work. Unfortunately, eight months later the business closed. She was retiring and moving to Florida. She figured she'd made enough money and was ready to retire at the ripe old age of forty-five! I was out of a job.

"It wasn't until July of 1993 that I started working in law again. I had really missed it. I found a great job through a 'head-hunter' service paid by my employer to find a decent secretary. I completed a two-week probationary period during which I got to know the attorneys in the firm and they got to know me. By the end of the two weeks I had proved to them that I was more than capable of handling the responsibility, knew the field, knew the word processing programs, and was easy to get along with. I've been here for three years now."

Advice from Jennifer Franks

"It is extremely important to be organized. I find that I get the most accomplished if I've a set place for everything and can get my hands on it easily and quickly. The other most important trait is to be confident under pressure. There's nothing like blowing a deadline because you're panicking. That's taken a long time for me to develop, but it has come. I used to have a hard time switching gears into a pressure situation, but now I just put aside the secondary task and put all my focus on the deadline. It helps to take a moment or two to get the first project physically off your desk and organize yourself before delving into the 'rush' job.

"It's also extremely important to be able to prioritize. Attorneys often depend on their secretaries to be able to determine for themselves what will take priority. To do that you must have an understanding of where all the projects are in their completion and what their deadlines are and then be able to make a rational decision about what needs to get done first.

"It's these parts of the job that I take pride in being able to accomplish. It's made me a team player, someone I know the attorneys can count on when it really matters. I suppose that's why I like my job. I guess you could say I'm a people pleaser. And I think every secretary has to admit that first, before they go any further. It's not a glamorous job, by any means, but it's an extremely important one."

Gigi Starnes—Legal Secretary

Gigi Starnes worked as a legal secretary for a one-lawyer firm in the mid-eighties. She graduated from a business college with an executive secretary degree in 1960.

"My hours were from 8:00 A.M. to 5:30 P.M. My first duty was to open the office, relock the door, then type all phone messages that came in overnight. There were regularly several. Then I sorted and opened the mail, stacked it in order of importance, made ready the banking deposits, and paid the bills. Then I started transcribing tapes my boss left on my desk, which amounted to several each day.

"It was also my job to call my employer on mornings he wasn't already in the office to make sure he was aware of appointments and court appearances set for that day. I also was to remind him if he needed to wear a suit.

"Each client had a file, and each file was arranged in date order with the latest date on top. Frequently, something from the back of the file had to be removed and copied then returned to its proper place in the folder. While this was necessary, it was also time consuming. Some of the files were quite full, so finding a specific bit of information was very much like finding a needle in a haystack. But there was a feeling of accomplishment when the bit was finally found. I also had to become a notary public and witness a variety of signings.

"Being responsible for knowing when to unlock the door to someone was quite a disturbing part of my job. I didn't know all the clients, nor did I know the normal routine for service and delivery personnel. My first day on the job, the bell rang and my boss asked me who was there. When I told him, he ran over to my desk and pointed to the bottom drawer. I opened it and saw a handgun. 'You do know how to shoot, don't you?' he asked. When I answered in the affirmative, he opened the door and had a rather nasty verbal exchange with an unhappy client. My boss had been a policeman in earlier days and had put himself through law school. His philosophy was that every person deserved a fair trial, and he often took clients other lawyers wouldn't represent. While most of his clients were fine people, I have to admit that a few of them scared the liver out of me.

"My boss would call frequently from his office for me to bring certain forms to him, and he would abbreviate their names.

'Bring me a TRO' (temporary restraining order), or a WF (will form), and a variety of others. One that had me stumped, however, was when he called, 'Bring me a DP.' I looked through the forms and could not find anything fitting the abbreviation. Finally, in shame, I went to him and admitted I didn't know what a DP was. He looked at me oddly and replied, 'It's a Dr. Pepper.'

"My responsibilities included filing papers at the courthouse, picking up and delivering papers, making sure dates were correct and that procedures were followed.

"I also was responsible for maintaining our law library, filing new additions to each volume, keeping all subscriptions in an orderly manner and all volumes in their proper places. This was tedious work but I learned a lot. The more I worked with the library, the more quickly I could find needed information.

"There was more work in one day than I could handle. No two days were ever the same; each brought a new problem to be solved, a new client to serve, a new task to learn. While this is what made the job interesting and challenging, it's also what made it exhausting and stressful."

How Gigi Starnes Got Started

"I worked as a secretary, file supervisor, PBX and radio operator, for Humble Oil & Refining Company, now Exxon. I stopped working for a salary to raise four children and held a variety of jobs during those years. When my last child finished high school, I decided to reenter the job market. In preparation for this, I attended community college and completed thirty-six hours, maintaining a 4.0 grade average.

"Once I decided to reenter the job market, I applied for several secretarial jobs that were offered in the newspaper, all of which I was qualified for. After submitting my resume, I was called for interviews at every place I'd applied. Somehow, a job wasn't offered. It finally dawned on me that my age was definitely a factor. (Even though we all know that's not supposed to happen, the reality is, it does.) So I branched out and began applying for a variety of jobs, some of which I was not qualified for. And that is how I became a legal secretary.

"I was called one morning to appear for an interview that afternoon. The law offices were in a seedy part of town, and the door was locked when I arrived. After identifying myself, I was buzzed in. The current secretary gave me a spelling test and a tape to transcribe. When that was finished, she took both in to the attorney. After a few minutes, she returned and ushered me into his inner sanctum. He was wearing a black silk shirt and about a pound and a half of gold chains. He was chain-smoking, and he was drinking some sort of darkish liquid out of a shot glass.

"The interview was informal and the work sounded interesting and challenging. I was questioned not only about my skills but was also asked to respond to various what-would-you-do-if . . . questions. At the end of a two-hour interview, the attorney, who was much younger than I, looked rather sadly into my eyes and said, 'Well, Mrs. Starnes, I guess I've finally started growing up today. You're hired. You're the oldest secretary I've ever had.'

"I was hired and was asked to begin work the following morning. When I arrived, my new boss pointed to my desk and handed me several tapes to transcribe. I was told to answer the phone 'Law offices' and take all messages. He said he was sure I could figure out his filing system then pointed to a mountain of papers. 'Everything has a name on it, just go by that and file the latest date on top,' he said. 'The mail is over there. Sort it by letters from clients, payments from clients, letters pertaining to cases, bills to be paid, and then the rest. Any checks take out, stamp, and get a deposit ready. You'll take a deposit to the bank every day. You'll also pay all the bills and keep the accounting books balanced.'

"That was the sum total of my training."

Advice from Gigi Starnes

"If you're considering becoming a legal secretary, there are some things you can do to prepare yourself. First of all, learn the lingo. Every profession has its own terminology, and you'll be miles ahead if you already know what to listen for. Have at your side an instant word guide for law and a copy of the *Legal Secretary's Handbook*.

"Be aware that part of your job is hearing sensitive and confidential information and that you have a responsibility to keep it to yourself. You will carry tremendous responsibility on your shoulders—your attorneys and their clients depend on you.

"The rewards are great. Not only are you well paid, but as a legal secretary, you stand tall in your profession. If you're good at your job, you are held in high esteem by important people and are given as much responsibility as you are willing to assume. While there are routine tasks to perform, the work is never dull—ever-changing problems cross your desk daily."

CHAPTER SEVEN

Law Enforcement Officers

F or those interested in the enforcement side of the law, there are many avenues to explore. From police officer to FBI agent, from U.S. Customs official to homicide detective, you can find the kind of work that would appeal to you most.

Jobs for Law Enforcement Officers

Police Officers and Detectives

Police officers and detectives who work in small communities and rural areas have many duties. In the course of a day's work, they may direct traffic at the scene of a fire, investigate a burglary, or give first aid to an accident victim. In a large police department, by contrast, officers usually are assigned to a specific type of duty. Most officers are detailed either to patrol or to traffic duty; smaller numbers are assigned to special work such as accident prevention. Others are experts in chemical and microscopic analysis, firearms identification, and handwriting or fingerprint identification. In very large cities, officers may be assigned to special task forces such as homicide, burglary, or even SWAT teams.

Detectives and Special Agents

Detectives and special agents are plainclothes investigators who gather facts and collect evidence for criminal cases. They conduct interviews, examine records, observe the activities of suspects, and participate in raids or arrests.

Federal Bureau of Investigation (FBI) Special Agents

FBI agents investigate violations of federal laws in connection with bank robbery, theft of government property, organized crime, espionage, sabotage, kidnapping, and terrorism. Agents with specialized training usually work on cases related to their background. For example, agents with an accounting background may investigate white-collar crimes such as bank embezzlements or fraudulent bankruptcies and land deals. Frequently, agents must testify in court about cases that they investigate.

The U.S. Department of Treasury

The U.S. Department of Treasury employs special agents who work for the U.S. Customs Service; the Bureau of Alcohol, Tobacco, and Firearms; the U.S. Secret Service; and the Internal Revenue Service.

U.S. Customs Agents

Customs agents enforce laws to prevent smuggling of goods across U.S. borders.

Alcohol, Tobacco, and Firearms Agents

ATF agents might investigate suspected illegal sales of guns or the underpayment of taxes by a liquor or cigarette manufacturer.

U.S. Secret Service Agents

Secret Service agents protect the president, vice president, their immediate families, presidential candidates, ex-presidents, and foreign dignitaries visiting the United States. Secret Service agents also investigate counterfeiting, the forgery of government checks or bonds, and the fraudulent use of credit cards.

Internal Revenue Service Special Agents

IRS agents collect evidence against individuals and companies that are evading the payment of Federal taxes.

Federal Drug Enforcement Agents

Drug Enforcement Administration (DEA) agents conduct criminal investigations of illicit drug activity. They compile evidence and arrest individuals who violate federal drug laws. They may prepare reports that are used in criminal proceedings, give testimony in court, and develop evidence that justifies the seizure of financial assets gained from illegal activity.

What It's Really Like

Ramesh Nyberg—Homicide Detective

Ramesh Nyberg is a homicide detective with the Metro-Dade Police Department in Miami, Florida. He began his career in 1979.

"I don't think there's any greater weapon in a policeman's arsenal than his own ears and his ability to listen. In street police work, when you're a uniformed police officer, you have to be very aware of what people are doing and saying. You can't take a report from people without listening to them. For purposes of your own safety, you have to listen carefully to what they're saying, their tone of voice, whether it's rising or falling. I think young police officers miss this a lot, but there are things people say and things they won't say that they'll only hint at, whether consciously or subconsciously. They have the potential to tell you a lot of things, but without your asking the proper questions, they won't say anything.

"This becomes even more important in detective work. Our interviews in homicide are very thorough. One thing we do in homicide that people don't see on television very often is that, while some detectives are working inside the house or the crime scene, other detectives will be knocking on every door on that block and possibly the next block. Very often people will see things, hear things, or know things, but they won't say a word until someone knocks on their door. Maybe a week later, we'll try a block a little farther away that we hadn't tried earlier, and we'll knock on people's doors there. And a little old lady will be in there and say, 'Oh, I heard a gunshot and saw a black car leaving.' We ask her why she didn't tell anybody. Her answer: 'Nobody asked me.' That's very common, and very often, too, the murderer might live in the neighborhood or the murderer might already be known and somebody next door might know something about it. 'Yeah, I remember last week him talking about killin' his wife. He's been complaining about her all week.' We encounter that type of thing.

"Here's something else that's important that you don't see in the movies or on television. When you make an arrest, the case is only beginning. On TV after the arrest, it's over. You get the closing credits while everyone is slapping each other on the back and going out for a beer. That's not the way it happens in police work. Very often when an arrest is made, a whole new avenue of the case opens up.

"If you're working a case where you have an unknown offender, you've got a dead body and that's it, the first thing you do is start with the victim. You try to find out who the victim's friends, enemies, lovers, relatives, coworkers were—everything about the victim you possibly can. You're looking for reasons why this person is dead and who would have the best opportunity, means, and motive to kill him.

"But you can't even begin guessing about motive until you know where the victim's haunts are and who he or she doesn't trust, and so on. Once you start working that whole circle around the victim, let's say you develop a suspect, and you sit down with that person and he confesses. Or for whatever reasons, you're able to identify the killer. Once you've made that identification, you then have another whole circle to investigate—his or her family, friends, coworkers. You might have to get search warrants for the suspect's car or house. He took a trip to Boston a week after the homicide? Let's see who he visited there, what he might have told that person. Oh, an ex-girlfriend? Let's go talk to her. You can't in good conscience omit that. There's only a small chance he told her anything, but you have to follow the lead. I've had to travel a lot in the course of my work. I've even been to other countries—Jamaica, Costa Rica, Canada. Miami is such a transient area. Our department is probably much more generous with travel budgets than others.

"What you want to do in a homicide case is get as much evidence against the suspect as possible. These cases are so heavily scrutinized—if you've watched one-tenth of the O. J. Simpson trial—well, that's typical of a homicide case. The defense tries to discredit everything and everybody that the state puts up. You've got to have overkill, you've got to have more than enough evidence in a homicide case. If you get two or three people who say, 'Oh yeah, I saw him do it,' you still have to look for four or five other witnesses who can say the same thing. You might have enough to make an arrest, but to convict you have to continue to try to get more."

Metro-Dade's Cold-Case Squad

Ramesh Nyberg is currently on the cold-case squad, handling old, unsolved murders.

"Cold cases or active investigations—each has its advantages. There's a real thrill to getting a fresh case and going out and working it, developing leads and seeing it progress. You can't really match that thrill. But it's also very hard on the family life. You're doing it all the time, you're always getting called out, and it's very taxing.

"With cold cases, you're on a different schedule. You can work until five then go home and have a more stable lifestyle. For my purposes, I prefer this assignment now.

"We have five detectives and a sergeant on our squad and we're actively working ten to fifteen cases. There are over a thousand waiting, but our success rate is not bad at all. Since 1982 or 1983, I think we've closed 120 cases. Since I've been on the squad, we've closed quite a few. It's a good feeling to go back and work a case that, for whatever reasons, wasn't solved earlier. And it's not that the detectives assigned to the original case didn't do a good job. It's always a question of time. When you're dealing with active cases, there's always another case given to you to juggle. We don't have to do that. We're not interrupted. When we make an appointment with a witness, we're able to keep it. We have the luxury of time to work on the case.

"I enjoy the ongoing challenge of trying to track down homicides. Homicide is the worst crime there is, and I like the fact we can work on cases that have no statute of limitations. That old cliché 'getting away with murder' is not really true.

"I don't envy robbery detectives. They work very hard, but often it's for naught. They're able to find the offenders, but often nothing happens to them in the court system. Robbers are getting these ridiculously light sentences. It's not until they actually kill someone that they get any real time."

The Stresses of Police Work

"I think the criminal justice system is one of the biggest gen-erators of stress in our work. Having to deal with a system that has been created and manipulated by attorneys is a very diffi-cult system to deal with. And here's one of the great myths that Hollywood has created: that there's this big, cooperative effort between police, court, and prosecutors; that it's all one big en-gine that's geared toward putting people in prison. But it's not like that at all. The prosecutors have their own agenda, and it's not our agenda at all. Their agenda is to move cases and to try only cases that are winnable. Our agenda is to get these people off the street. They don't want marginal cases. And there are times you can't help that. There are times when we have enough probable cause to arrest someone. He's a hazard and we need to get him off the street. Prosecuting him might be difficult, we might lose, but let's go for it. We might win. You're constantly arguing your position, and that creates stress. The justice sys-tem in general is not just pro-law enforcement.

"Then there's the bureaucratic nature of police departments. The way we work is not what you'd find in a modern, success-ful, growing corporation that is constantly striving for excel-lence. And I don't mean this to demean the department; it's an excellent one. But it's the nature of the infrastructure of police work. We have, for example, a department that has a lot of money. But sometimes the money is spent on things that are not directly applied to bettering investigations. I think if you look at what the most important investigations are—sexual batteries, homicides, robberies—you want to give those people the best equipment and resources so they can do their work. Instead, the money goes to bigger cars for the chiefs, cellular phones to put in those cars. The detectives don't get enough phones or cars, and so we see some of the money being wasted. And you see the department much more concerned with pre-senting some sort of veiled public image rather than really do-ing the best possible work we can.

"The actual physical part of seeing bodies shot up and cut up, or whatever, is something you learn how to handle pretty fast. You get over that initial shock after seeing it three or four times. It becomes pretty routine. A bludgeoned or dismembered body becomes nothing more than another piece of evidence. We learn how to go into a certain mode when we're at a crime scene, to look at these things objectively and without emotion. But I think it does affect us. You can't totally disregard the natural human feeling of being revolted or infuriated by a lot of things you see.

"I think this particularly happens when it comes to innocent victims. But we don't see a lot of innocent victims. A lot of people we deal with put themselves in bad positions. The majority of our victims are drug dealers, robbers, swindlers, people who are out there committing crimes themselves. What you hear on the news—the child accidentally shot in a drive-by, the tourist stabbed, the suburban housewife murdered—actually represents only a small fragment of our victims. These are widely publicized because they're shocking stories, and people can relate to these victims, but the news doesn't tend to report the onslaught of cases we get where one crack dealer kills another or a smuggler dies shot, bound, and gagged in the trunk of a car. They don't hold the same emotional level that other cases do.

"Cases involving children affect people a lot, and we're no different that way. We're no more able to shrug that off than any other average person. Some of us might fool ourselves into thinking we can, but we can't.

"We have a child exploitation unit, but I don't think I could work that. I happen to have a very sensitive spot with children. I would not be able to handle that emotionally for very long.

"There's not nearly as much danger as you see on television. Homicide detectives don't get into running gun battles as often as they do on television shows. It's really a pretty safe job. When we get to a crime scene, the crime is over. There are uniformed officers standing over it, the scene has been roped off and secured.

"Going to interview a suspect, however, could be dangerous. If we know the person we're going to interview is a suspect, depending on the level of contact we're going to have with him, we'll govern ourselves accordingly. We'll say, 'This guy probably did it; he looks like a good candidate.' Then we'll take two detectives, maybe three, to make our first contact, to feel him out, and to see what he says or how he reacts. If it's someone we're planning to arrest, that's a different story. We'll go in with more people. On rare occasions, we might get surprised by someone we didn't think of as a suspect. We go to interview a neighbor, for example, who turns out to be the offender.

"That's why we always are on our guard and we never work alone. There's a lot more interaction going on about decisions that have to be made—with meetings among the detectives and between the detectives and the prosecutors—than you see on television. We do everything strategically. We are always trying to anticipate what we're going to face in court, and we try to decide ahead of time what the right strategies are we'll follow. That TV image of the lone cop going off on his own is pure fantasy. You don't have detectives working a homicide by themselves. I love *Columbo* and how at the end he always describes his train of thought and what led him to the suspect. But it just doesn't work that way.

"As far as corruption, I can speak for myself and the rest of my squad. We don't have any time for corruption. I think I'd give that about half a second. I think you make your decision—you're either going to be a crook or a cop. Don't try to be both. I'd probably have less contempt for someone who's just an all-out crook, than somebody who is a police officer and wants to be a crook at the same time. That person I could really hate.

"Another part of police work you don't see is the constant joking and camaraderie. I don't think you could survive without it. The work is so intensely serious and the topics we deal with are so grim, sometimes, so if you're constantly taking it to heart you'd have a lot of tension in the workplace. We're constantly finding ways to break the tension."

How Ramesh Nyberg Got Started

"It was not one of these things that I always wanted to be a policeman as a kid. I remember that I wanted to be a bus driver. I didn't really gain a keen interest in police work until I was about eighteen. I was attending Miami-Dade Community College and I used to study with a friend who listened to a police scanner. It fascinated me, and I decided to sign up for an observer ride. When I was out there with them and saw what the police did firsthand, how they utilized all their senses, not just their authority, but their intellect, too, it really interested me a lot. Two or three observer rides later, I was pretty much hooked on the idea of police work as a profession.

"Through word of mouth and through the paper I learned which departments were hiring, and I started putting in my applications. My first receptive response was from Opalocka, and that's where I started out. Opalocka sent me to the police academy, which at the time was held at the north campus of Miami-Dade Community College. It's called the Southeast Florida Institute of Criminal Justice. At that time the program was five and a half months. Now I think it's up to eight months.

"I stayed at Opalocka for one year, then I moved to the North Miami Police Department and was there for two years, from 1980 to 1982. But I was getting tired of small police departments. Opalocka was a thirty-three-officer department; North Miami had about ninety. The opportunities to move around and do different kinds of police work, such as detective work, were much more scarce.

"With the county, there are any number of detective bureaus to move around in. It's a police force of three thousand-plus. There are many more options. In 1982 I was able to transfer to Metro-Dade. I had to stay on patrol for almost three years, going out on a range of calls, covering the beat. In 1985 I was made a detective."

Do You Have What It Takes?

"This job requires that you have a certain personality," Ramesh Nyberg explains. "You have to be flexible, tenacious, and have convictions. If you don't, then what are you doing there?

"There are times in homicide when you almost have to forget you're a cop. If you're sitting down with someone and conducting an intimate interview, you cannot let your authority get in your way. You can't get offended or react the way a typical young cop on the street would react. If someone calls you a pig, for example, you can't have a macho response. And I mean that to apply to both men and women.

"It's a thing about the badge. If you get insulted on the street, you can't back down because you'll be perceived as weak. And people will try to take advantage of you. In the interview room, you have to be more on their level to be effective. You have to get them to trust you. To do that, you have to be able to put your emotions aside.

"Police work really involves just hard work and determination, observation, and common sense. I think that when people watch television shows about police work, they see cops as beings with some sort of special powers. And I think people who want to become police officers and do become police officers are special people in many ways, but it's simply a matter of applying yourself and being objective. You can't get too locked into one train of thought.

"If you enter this profession, don't expect to change too much. A lot of cops think they're going to be able to change people. You might affect a couple of people's lives, but basically, we're not going to change crime, we're not going to stop drugs. I don't think it's a fatalistic attitude; I think it's just reality. On the bright side, we're always going to have a job."

"This is my career and I love my career, but it's not my life. I think you should have other interests to keep yourself on an even keel."

Ramesh Nyberg has followed his own advice. He makes time in his busy schedule to work at freelance writing and has sold numerous articles to magazines, including the "Ten Most Common Crime Writing Mistakes" to *Writer's Digest*. He has just finished a novel and is in the process of submitting it to an agent.

Undercover Cops

Timothy Bronson—Detective Sergeant

While homicide detectives almost never work undercover, there are many other units that utilize clandestine means to accomplish their goals—catching the bad guys. Detective Sergeant Timothy Bronson has been with the Fort Lauderdale Police Department in Florida since 1981. Many of those years he worked undercover in specialized tactical units. He also worked on the SWAT team.

"I was a great reader of mysteries when I was kid, anything to do with serial killers, rapists, that sort of thing. And I think that's how the seed got planted.

"I got a job as a security guard in California and I was on the list to take the LAPD test, but then all of a sudden there was a hiring freeze. My father called to tell me that my hometown, Little Falls, New York, was giving the test. That was in 1977. I started as a patrolman, but I wanted to work for a bigger police department. In 1981 I started looking around. I got hired in Palm Beach County and in Baltimore, then Fort Lauderdale.

"When I started in Fort Lauderdale, I worked the midnight shift for a year and a half, then went into the tactical unit, which is a plainclothes undercover unit. We tried to get robberies in progress, apprehend rapists, that sort of thing.

"In 1985 Domino's Pizza guys were being robbed. The offender was calling in for pizza, then when the driver showed up, he'd put a gun under the guy's chin. To catch him, I posed as a Domino's delivery man. I got Officer of the Year for that.

"Our unit would cover burglaries, too, and if another agency called looking for a violent fugitive, we'd go after him. When the Rollover Rapist was on the loose back in 1985, we saturated the area looking for him, and we caught him. We'd use female decoys and simulate a car breakdown to see what happened.

"I've hidden in dumpsters and gotten into a few close calls. One time I was trying to put a 'bird dog'—that's a tracking device—on a rape suspect's car. I crawled under the car, which was in his driveway at the time, but before I finished, he came walking out and got into his car. He almost ran me over—he started to back up, but my partners came and distracted him by asking for directions. I was able to get out in time.

"That wasn't the first time we staged distractions. One time two cops had an accident—they ran their cars into each other—so we could distract a suspect and go in and get him.

"From 1983 to 1988 I worked with the SWAT teams. We had two teams, entry teams, of four guys each. We'd go into buildings after barricaded subjects, or to carry out search warrants, or on narcotics busts.

"When the President came to town, we guarded him. At the funeral for a cop, we handled the security. We'd be on the rooftops making sure that no one was there, ready to fire into the crowd.

"The camaraderie in this work is unbelievable. There were fourteen in our unit, and all would lay down their lives for you. I knew that if I was running down the hallway chasing someone, they'd be right behind me.

"But those were rough days, and there was a lot of drinking after work to deal with the stress. I think back to what I did: I was a fool, I was young, and I had the attitude I would never get hurt. I've been asked to go back to the SWAT team as sergeant, but I turned it down. My wife didn't appreciate my being called in the middle of the night. I was glad to move on to another assignment."

The Ride of Your Life

If you are willing to sign an agreement that the police department will be held harmless in case of any "incidents," you could find yourself riding shotgun in a police car. Most every department across the country allows what are called *observer rides*. Interested parties spend a whole shift with an officer of the law, going out on any calls that happen to come in.

What would your night be like? Here are some of the possibilities: in-progress calls, delayed calls, domestic violence, robberies, drug busts—even homicides.

All sorts of people take advantage of observer rides—people just like yourself, law and criminal justice students, writers, career investigators, and even private citizens who are concerned about their communities. To arrange an observer ride, telephone the media relations department or the public information office of your local police department.

Training

Civil service regulations govern the appointment of police and detectives in practically all states and large cities and in many small ones. Candidates must be U.S. citizens, usually at least twenty years of age, and must meet rigorous physical and personal qualifications. Eligibility for appointment depends on performance in competitive written examinations as well as on education and experience. Physical examinations often include tests of vision, strength, and agility.

Because personal characteristics such as honesty, good judgment, and a sense of responsibility are especially important in police and detective work, candidates are interviewed by a senior officer at police headquarters, and their character traits and background are investigated. In some police departments, candidates also may be interviewed by a psychiatrist or a psychologist or be given a personality test. Most applicants are subjected to lie-detector examinations and drug testing. Some police departments subject police officers in sensitive positions to drug testing as a condition of continuing employment.

In large police departments, where most jobs are found, applicants usually must have a high school education. An increasing number of cities and states require some college training, and some hire law enforcement students as police interns; some departments require a college degree. A few police departments accept applicants as recruits who have less than a high school education, particularly if they have worked in a field related to law enforcement.

To be considered for appointment as an FBI special agent, an applicant either must be a graduate of an accredited law school; be a college graduate with a major in either accounting, engineering, or computer science; or be a college graduate with either fluency in a foreign language or three years of full-time work experience. Applicants must be U.S. citizens, between twenty-three and thirty-five years of age at the time of appointment, and willing to accept an assignment anywhere in the United States. They also must be in excellent physical condition with at least 20/200 vision corrected to 20/40 in one eye and 20/20 in the other eye. All new agents undergo fifteen weeks of training at the FBI academy at the U.S. Marine Corps base in Quantico, Virginia.

Applicants for special-agent jobs with the U.S. Department of Treasury must have a bachelor's degree or a minimum of three years of work experience, of which at least two must be in criminal investigation. Candidates must be in excellent physical condition and be less than thirty-five years of age at the time they enter duty. Treasury agents undergo eight weeks of training at the Federal Law Enforcement Training Center in Glynco, Georgia, and another eight weeks of specialized training with their particular bureau.

Applicants for special-agent jobs with the U.S. Drug Enforcement Administration (DEA) must have a college degree in any field and either one year of experience conducting criminal investigations or have achieved a record of scholastic excellence while in college. The minimum age for entry is twenty-one and the maximum age is thirty-six. Drug enforcement agents undergo fourteen weeks of specialized training at the FBI Academy in Quantico, Virginia.

More and more, police departments are encouraging applicants to take post-high school training in law enforcement. Many entrants to police and detective jobs have completed some formal postsecondary education, and a significant number are college graduates. Many junior colleges, colleges, and universities offer programs in law enforcement or administration of justice. Other courses helpful in preparing for a police career include psychology, counseling, English, American history, public administration, public relations, sociology, business law, chemistry, and physics. Participation in physical education and sports is especially helpful in developing the stamina and agility needed for police work. Knowledge of a foreign language is an asset in areas that have concentrations of ethnic populations.

Some large cities hire high school graduates who are still in their teens as civilian police cadets or trainees. They do clerical work and attend classes and are appointed to the regular force at age twenty-one, if qualified.

Before their first assignments, officers usually go through a period of training. In small communities, recruits work for a short time with experienced officers. In state and large city police departments, officers get more formal training that may last a number of weeks or months. This training includes class-room instruction in constitutional law and civil rights, state laws and local ordinances, and accident investigation. Recruits also receive training and supervised experience in patrol, traf-fic control, firearms, self-defense, first aid, and emergency management.

Police officers usually become eligible for promotion after a probationary period ranging from six months to three years. In a large department, promotion may enable an officer to become a detective or specialize in one type of police work such as labo-ratory analysis of evidence, traffic control, communications, or working with juveniles. Promotions to sergeant, lieutenant, and captain usually are made according to a candidate's position on a promotion list, as determined by scores on a written exami-nation and on-the-job performance.

Many types of training help police officers and detectives improve their job performance. Through training given at po-lice department academies required annually in many states and colleges, officers keep abreast of crowd-control techniques, civil defense, legal developments that affect their work, and ad-vances in law enforcement equipment. Many police depart-ments pay all or part of the tuition for officers to work toward associate and bachelor's degrees in law enforcement, police science, administration of justice, or public administration, and pay higher salaries to those who earn degrees.

Job Outlook

Employment of police officers, detectives, and special agents is expected to increase more slowly than the average for all occupations through the year 2005. A more security-conscious society and growing concern about drug-related crimes should contribute to the increasing demand for police services. How-ever, employment growth will be tempered somewhat by continuing budgetary constraints faced by law enforcement agencies. In addition, private security firms may increasingly assume some routine police duties such as crowd surveillance at airports and other public places. Although turnover in police, detective, and special-agent jobs is among the lowest of all occupations, the need to replace workers who retire, transfer to other occupations, or stop working for other reasons will be the source of most job openings.

The opportunity for public service through police work is attractive to many. The job frequently is challenging and involves much responsibility. Furthermore, in many communities, police officers may retire with a pension to pursue a second career while still in their forties. Because of attractive salaries and benefits, the number of qualified candidates generally exceeds the number of job openings in many federal agencies and some state and local police departments, resulting in increased hiring standards and selectivity by employers. Competition is expected to remain keen for higher-paying jobs in larger police departments. Persons having college training in law enforcement should have the best opportunities. Opportunities will be best in those communities whose departments are expanding and are having difficulty attracting an adequate supply of police officers.

Competition is expected to be extremely keen for special-agent positions with the FBI, Treasury Department, and Drug Enforcement Administration, as these prestigious jobs tend to attract a far greater number of applicants than the number of job openings. Consequently, only the most highly qualified candidates will obtain jobs.

The level of government spending influences the employment of police officers, detectives, and special agents. The number of job opportunities, therefore, can vary from year to year and from place to place. Layoffs, on the other hand, are rare because early retirements enable most staffing cuts to be handled through attrition. Police officers who lose their jobs from budget cuts usually have little difficulty finding jobs with other police departments.

Salaries

In 1994, the median salary of nonsupervisory police officers and detectives was about $34,000 a year. The middle 50 percent earned between about $25,500 and $43,900; the lowest-paid 10 percent were paid less than $17,900, while the highest-paid 10 percent earned over $56,100 a year. Generally, salaries tend to be higher in larger, more urban jurisdictions that usually have bigger police departments.

Police officers and detectives in supervisory positions had a median salary of about $42,800 a year, also in 1994. The middle 50 percent earned between about $30,100 and $52,500; the lowest-paid 10 percent were paid less than $19,800, while the highest-paid 10 percent earned over $62,100 annually.

Sheriffs, bailiffs, and other law enforcement officers had a median annual salary of about $26,800 in 1994. The middle 50 percent earned between about $20,800 and $37,200; the lowest-paid 10 percent were paid less than $16,500, while the highest-paid 10 percent earned over $48,600.

In 1995, FBI agents started at about $31,200 a year, while Treasury Department agents started at about $23,200 or $28,300 a year, and DEA agents at either $22,700 or $27,800 a year, depending on their qualifications. Salaries of experienced FBI agents started at around $47,900, while supervisory agents started at around $56,600 a year. Salaries of experienced Treasury Department and DEA agents started at $61,100, while supervisory agents started at $66,800. Federal agents may, however, be eligible for a special law enforcement compensation and retirement plan; applicants should ask their recruiter for more information.

Total earnings frequently exceed the stated salary due to payments for overtime, which can be significant, especially during criminal investigations or when police are needed for crowd control during sporting events or political rallies. In addition to the common fringe benefits of paid vacation, sick leave, and medical and life insurance, most police departments and federal agencies provide officers with special allowances for uniforms and furnish revolvers, nightsticks, handcuffs, and other required equipment. In addition, because police officers generally are covered by liberal pension plans, many retire at half pay after twenty or twenty-five years of service.

CHAPTER EIGHT

Private Investigators

P rivate detectives and investigators assist attorneys, government agencies, businesses, and the public with a variety of problems such as gathering facts, tracing debtors, or conducting background investigations. The main job of private investigators and some detectives is to obtain information and locate assets or individuals. Some private investigators protect stores and hotels from theft, vandalism, and disorder.

About half of all private investigators are self-employed or work for detective agencies. They also find work either full-time or as independent contractors with insurance companies, shopping malls, hotels, or other private concerns. They can work under cover, infiltrating a ring of thieves, or sit at a desk doing background checks. They sniff out shoplifters, finger employees who are stealing, or locate missing persons. They also act as bodyguards or security guards.

Private investigators working as general investigators have duties ranging from locating missing persons to exposing fraudulent worker's compensation claims. Some investigators specialize in one field, such as finance, where they might use accounting skills to investigate the financial standing of a company or locate funds stolen by an embezzler.

Many investigators spend considerable time conducting surveillance, seeking to observe inconsistencies in a person's behavior. For example, a person who has filed a worker's compensation claim that an injury has made walking difficult should not be able to jog or mow the lawn. If such behavior is observed, the investigator takes video or still photographs to document the activity and reports back to the supervisor or client.

Some investigations involve verification of facts, such as an individual's place of employment or income. This might involve a phone call or a visit to the workplace. In other investigations, especially in missing persons cases, the investigator interviews people to learn as much as possible about someone's previous movements.

Types of Investigators

Legal Investigators

Legal investigators specialize in cases involving the courts and lawyers. To assist in preparing criminal defenses, investigators locate witnesses, interview police, gather and review evidence, take photographs, and testify in court. In addition, they might perform the same or similar functions working with prosecutors preparing their cases.

Arson Investigators

Arson investigators generally work for fire departments but also cooperate with local police departments and often testify in court. They start out as fully trained firefighters before moving into an investigator's role.

Not all fire investigators work for fire departments. Some, with the appropriate training and experience, find work with insurance companies or private investigation firms.

Corporate Investigators

Corporate investigators work for companies other than investigative firms—often large corporations. They conduct external and internal investigations. External investigations focus on preventing criminal schemes, thefts of company assets, and fraudulent deliveries of products by suppliers. Internal investigations ensure that expense accounts are not abused and employees are not stealing.

Financial Investigators

Financial investigators may be hired to investigate the financial standing of companies or individuals. These investigators often work with investment bankers and lawyers. They generally develop confidential financial profiles of individuals or companies that may be party to large financial transactions. An asset search is a common type of such an investigation.

Store Detectives

Private detectives and investigators who work for large retail stores or malls are responsible for loss control and asset protection. They detect theft by shoplifters, vendor representatives, delivery personnel, and even store employees. Store detectives also conduct periodic inspections of stock areas, dressing rooms, and rest rooms and sometimes assist in the opening and closing of the store. They may prepare loss-prevention and security reports for management and testify in court against persons they apprehend.

Training

Most employers prefer to hire high school graduates, and a growing number of states are enacting mandatory training programs for investigators. You can get entry-level training on the job. Many come to the profession from related fields—former police officers or government agents, or military personnel—or from such diverse professions as finance, accounting, investigative reporting, insurance, and law.

The vast majority of states and the District of Columbia require licenses for private investigators. In most cases, it is the state police department that issues the licenses, but requirements vary widely.

Some states have very liberal requirements. Others, such as California, have stringent regulations. For example, the California Department of Consumer Affairs Bureau of Security and Investigative Services requires six thousand hours of investigative experience, a background check, a qualifying score on a written examination, payment of a $50 application fee and a $32 fingerprint fee, and payment of an annual $175 license fee upon approval.

A college degree, especially in criminal justice or related fields, is becoming more and more the preferred background in some companies.

An understanding of computers is also important for investigators. Computers have changed the nature of this profession and have become an integral part of investigative work. They allow investigators to obtain massive amounts of information in a short period of time from the dozens of online databases containing probate records, motor-vehicle registrations, credit reports, association membership lists, and other information.

Job Outlook

Employment of private detectives and investigators is expected to grow much faster than the average for all occupations through the year 2005. In addition, job turnover should create many additional job openings, particularly among wage and salaried workers. Nevertheless, competition is expected to be high for the available openings because careers as private detectives or investigators are attractive to many people.

Salaries

James Rockford asked for $200 a day plus expenses. In real life, P.I.s bill their clients anywhere from $25 to $125 per hour, depending upon the type of investigation. Beginning investigators working for a private firm might start out only in the teens. Earnings vary greatly depending upon the employer, the specialty, and geographic area. Experienced investigators can earn anywhere from $20,000 a year to $300,000. Those who own their own firms and are doing well make at the higher end; those who work as store detective, for example, see the bottom of the scale. According to a study by Abbott, Langer & Associates, private investigators averaged about $36,700 a year in 1993, and store detectives about $16,100.

What It's Really Like

Joe Nickell—Undercover Investigator

More than twenty years ago Joe Nickell began his career as a private investigator for a world-famous detective agency. He has since taken another track and is now a paranormal investigator. But he got his start doing surveillance, background checks, and some dicey undercover work.

"I did mostly undercover jobs. Between those jobs, there were all sorts of surveillance work and background checks. I was even a bodyguard for a politician. But primarily, I was a part of the cadre of young investigators doing the more dangerous undercover work.

"We would work in a company's warehouse—as a stock clerk, shipper/receiver, mail clerk, fork lift driver—wherever they could slip us in. Our job was really to become aware of and infiltrate theft rings operating there. We'd set them up and bust them. The work was done privately and secretly. We'd assure the owners that we could get rid of the problem without the whole story coming out.

"If the story did come out, it would result in bad morale. The employees would not be happy that the bosses had sent spies in. The police would not be involved. The company would handle it themselves, fire the men, and hope to keep the thieves out.

"Plus, the detective agency would not want its men to have to go to court. Once you did, and you were identified, it would mean the end of your undercover career. The agency would want to be able to use us again and again, not just one time.

"I also did surveillance work, staking out a place where we had undercover guys. Or at times we'd be on the phone, just checking up on background and character of different people. Unlike some of the guys who hated doing any of the office work, I would go looking for the general work whenever I was between undercover assignments.

"When you were on an undercover assignment, you got your paycheck with the other factory or warehouse workers. Then your agency would make up the difference in your pay. You'd also get extra danger pay on top of that."

Insurance Fraud

Joe Nickell also worked on insurance fraud cases. "I was assigned to do surveillance on someone who was claiming he had a back injury. We staked out his house and watched him work on his car, photographing every move. He was bending over, darting up the steps two at a time. We documented it all."

Art Forgeries

This is not a field to enter into lightly. One must have a serious background in art, either as an artist, art gallery owner, or museum curator. Rarely is authenticating art a full-time position. It often comes as a sideline to regular duties in the above-mentioned occupations.

Matthew Carone—Art Gallery Owner and Forgery Investigator

Matthew Carone is the owner of the Carone Gallery, a prestigious establishment in Fort Lauderdale, Florida. He handles mainly contemporary art—American, some European, and some Latin American paintings and sculpture. His reputation became established, in part, as the result of discovering an art forgery.

"When you're starting, you have to establish yourself as a serious gallery. I happened to do it by way of master graphics. I got involved with original prints, not reproductions, but very serious Picassos, very serious Cézanne and Matisse prints, and I got a reputation for that in the early years. This made it easier for me to then work one-on-one with important artists because they knew of my seriousness.

"Many of the sources for these prints happened to be in Europe, which allowed me to go there every two or three months. The most important dealers in Europe met once a month to discuss what was happening in the art world—what was new, what was fake, that sort of thing. As it turned out, I had discovered a Picasso fake and got a lot of mileage and publicity through that.

"I'm color-blind, but I become value sensitive. I can see the value of a color, the lightness or darkness, more so than a person with normal color vision. The ink used for this one Picasso was called an ivory black, which is the blackest of blacks, but I knew that the originals had a warmer black. On the basis of that I knew there was something wrong, so I went to Paris and showed it to a very important Picasso dealer. He said to me, 'Mr. Carone, if you had showed me this print framed, under glass, I would have said it was okay, but you're right, this is a fake.' This led me to Picasso's biggest dealer, but my biggest mistake was when he said we must show this to Picasso—I should have insisted that I go along with that print, but I didn't do that. They sent it to him and Picasso did send it back to me with *Faux*, fake, and a line through it. But Picasso signed it, meaning 'Picasso says faux,' so it then achieved some value. Anything he put his name to had value and the faux print became an interesting thing to see. A prominent international auction house said that the print was very good, so whoever the artist was, he had a lot of talent. The fake was terrific.

"The FBI, of course, got involved with this; they had an idea who he was, but it was never pursued because it's very difficult to prove. They never found out.

"This event came at that time of my life when I was getting involved seriously, and it gave me a new level of importance. Everybody started banging on my door wanting me to look at their Picassos. Now, over the years I've developed a clientele that comes to me for particulars."

Chris Goodwin—Investigator

Chris Goodwin works as an investigator and office manager in the small solo-practice law firm owned by his wife, attorney M. J. Goodwin. (See Chapter 2.)

"I was a 'private' investigator at one time, when I was licensed and working for a private agency. It's not required to be licensed if you're only working for one person. If you're going to work for a firm that sends you out on different cases, then you'd need to be licensed. I'm called just 'investigator' now.

"One of my duties is to serve papers. Anytime somebody is being sued or getting a divorce, the papers have to be served in person. You can't just mail the papers with the court date on them; you have to actually hand them to the recipients. It involves a lot of time running around and trying to track people down.

"I've done things like follow cheating hearts around, taking their photos (in public places only—no Peeping Tom stuff). I also interview potential clients or current clients. It depends on what the case is. If it's a drug case, for example, and your client is in jail, you want to hear his or her side of the story. You'll already know the law enforcement side.

"Also, I occasionally interview witnesses in battered spouse cases. Right now I'm trying to find folks who've seen a man hit his wife, or have seen her bruises. The client usually provides names to us but is often mistaken about whether or not a person is a witness. Some clients think that if they tell a witness something, that person is a witness. But that's not the case. The person has to speak from personal observations. I also help the wives file restraining orders.

"In a current case, I am trying to find folks who can testify as to whom a child lived with during a certain period of time. In related work, I am trying to work out restitution with victims whose property was damaged by a drunk driver. In another criminal case, I am trying to line up and organize restitution for a client who wrote about forty-five bad checks.

"As an investigator, I don't really go around and try to find out 'whodunnit' to get my client off. That's for television—they always seem to find the actual person who did it. But basically, in real life, you're innocent until proven guilty. If you should happen to come up with the real culprit in the course of your investigation, then fine, but what we are more concerned with is trying to get evidence to clear our client, not necessarily to find out who did it. We interview people to establish alibis, for example. We work for the accused trying to clear them.

"There's no typical day—every day is different. Sometimes it's busy, sometimes slow. Today, for example, I called a few witnesses but couldn't find anyone in. It can be frustrating and, unfortunately, it is not very exciting, for the most part—not like what you see on TV.

"But I like the freedom my job gives me. I'm not stuck at a desk all day, and I don't do the same thing over and over. I have to be creative to solve problems."

How Chris Goodwin Got Started

"I became interested in investigative work later in life. My home was burglarized several years ago. Nobody really seemed to want to do anything about it. That bothered me, so I decided to learn more about law enforcement. I had to learn slowly; I couldn't quit my full-time job. I was working in the production lab at a chemical company as the senior lab technician, and I also worked in juvenile probation for about two years.

"I wanted to be in law enforcement, but my wife just couldn't stand the thought of that—too much life-threatening stuff. Investigative work seemed like the next-best thing. I approached the owner of a private detective agency and security firm and told him I was interested in the field. I didn't have any experience, but I was willing to learn and he took me under his wing.

"I got on-the-job training with an experienced investigator at the firm and I also attended seminars at the Criminal Justice Academy. They covered search and seizure, the laws of arrest, and public speaking and courtroom presentations. I am also a certified firearms instructor. The work there consisted mainly of divorce cases, trying to catch cheating spouses. I also did some repossession work.

"When my wife opened her law practice, we didn't know at first if it would take in enough income to support us both. But it did, and I was able to join her there in January 1996."

Expert Advice from Chris Goodwin

"Get with a pro and learn the ropes. It can be dangerous, and you need to know what to expect. A background in criminal justice can be helpful. You'll need to know the rules of evidence in order to obtain information that can be used in court.

"If you don't know what you are doing, you will not be able to effectively represent or help a client and may, in fact, do damage to the client's case. Having no investigator is better than having a bad one."

CHAPTER NINE

Corrections Officers

M any corrections officers guard prisoners in small municipal jails or precinct station houses, where their responsibilities are wide ranging, while others control inmates in large state and federal penitentiaries, where job duties are more specialized. A relatively small number guard aliens who are being held by the Immigration and Naturalization Service awaiting release or deportation.

Regardless of the setting, corrections officers maintain order within the institution, enforce rules and regulations, and often supplement the counseling that inmates receive from psychologists, social workers, and other mental health professionals.

To make sure inmates are orderly and obey rules, corrections officers monitor inmates' activities, including working, exercising, eating, and bathing. They assign and supervise inmates' work assignments, as well as instruct and help them on specific tasks. Sometimes it is necessary to search inmates and their living quarters for weapons or drugs, to settle disputes between inmates, and to enforce discipline. Corrections officers cannot show favoritism and must report any inmate who violates the rules. To prevent escapes, officers staff security positions in towers and at gates. They count inmates periodically to make sure all are present.

Corrections officers inspect the facilities to assure the safety and security of the prisoners. For example, they check cells and other areas of the institution for unsanitary conditions, fire hazards, and evidence of infractions of rules by inmates. In addition, they routinely inspect locks, window bars, grille doors, and gates for signs of tampering.

Corrections officers report orally and in writing on inmate conduct and on the quality and quantity of work done by inmates. Officers also report disturbances, violations of rules, and any unusual occurrences. They usually keep a daily record of their activities.

In some modern facilities, corrections officers monitor the activities of prisoners from a centralized control center with the aid of closed-circuit television cameras and a computer tracking system.

Within the institution, corrections officers escort inmates to and from cells and other areas and admit and accompany authorized visitors. They also escort prisoners between the institution and courtrooms, medical facilities, and other destinations. From time to time, they may inspect mail for contraband (prohibited items), administer first aid, or assist police authorities by investigating crimes committed within the institution and by searching for escaped inmates.

Counseling and helping inmates with problems are increasingly important parts of the corrections officer's job. Correctional institutions usually employ psychologists and social workers to counsel inmates, but corrections officers informally supplement the work of the professionals. They may arrange a change in a daily schedule so that an inmate can visit the library, help inmates get news of their families, talk over personal problems that may have led to committing a crime, or suggest where to look for a job after release from prison. In some institutions, officers receive specialized training and have a more formal counseling role and may lead or participate in group counseling sessions.

Corrections sergeants directly supervise corrections officers. They usually are responsible for maintaining security and directing the activities of a group of inmates during an assigned watch or in an assigned area.

Corrections officers may work indoors or outdoors, depending on their specific duties. Some indoor areas are well lighted, heated, and ventilated, but others are overcrowded, hot, and noisy. Outdoors, weather conditions may be disagreeable, for example, when standing watch on a guard tower in cold weather.

Working in a correctional institution can be stressful and hazardous; corrections officers occasionally have been injured or killed during inmate disturbances.

Corrections officers usually work an eight-hour day, five days a week. Prison security must be provided around the clock, which means some officers work weekends, holidays, and nights. In addition, officers may frequently be required to work overtime.

Training

Most institutions require that corrections officers meet an eighteen- or twenty-one-year age minimum, have a high school education or its equivalent, and be a United States citizen. In addition, correctional institutions increasingly seek corrections officers with postsecondary education in psychology, criminology, and related fields, reflecting a continuing emphasis on personal counseling and rehabilitation of inmates.

Corrections officers must be in good health. Many states require candidates to meet formal standards of physical fitness, eyesight, and hearing. Strength, good judgment, and the ability to think and act quickly are assets. Other common requirements include a driver's license, work experience that demonstrates reliability, and having no felony convictions. Some states screen applicants for drug abuse and require candidates to pass a written or oral examination.

Federal, state, and local departments of correction provide training for corrections officers based on guidelines established by the American Correctional Association, the American Jail Association, and other professional organizations. Some states

have special training academies. All states and local departments of correction provide informal on-the-job training and
advanced training as well.

Academy trainees generally receive several weeks or months
of instruction on institutional policies, regulations, and operations; counseling psychology, crisis intervention, inmate behavior, and contraband control; custody and security procedures;
fire and safety; inmate rules and rights; administrative responsibilities; written and oral communication, including preparation of reports; self-defense, including the use of firearms;
cardiopulmonary resuscitation; and physical fitness training.
New federal corrections officers undergo two weeks of training
at their assigned institutions followed by three weeks of basic
correctional instruction at the Federal Bureau of Prisons training center at Glynco, Georgia.

On-the-job trainees receive several weeks or months of similar training in an actual job setting under an experienced officer. Experienced officers receive in-service training to keep
abreast of new ideas and procedures. Some complete home-
study courses.

With additional education, experience, or training, qualified
officers may advance to corrections sergeant or other supervisory, administrative, or counseling positions. Many correctional
institutions require experience as a corrections officer for other
corrections positions. Officers sometimes transfer to related
areas, such as probation and parole.

Job Outlook

Job opportunities for corrections officers are expected to be
plentiful through the year 2005. The need to replace corrections officers who transfer to other occupations or leave the
labor force, coupled with rising employment demand, will generate tens of thousands of job openings each year. Correctional

institutions have traditionally experienced some difficulty in attracting qualified applicants, and this situation is expected to continue, ensuring highly favorable job prospects.

Employment of corrections officers is expected to increase much faster than the average for all occupations through the year 2005 as additional officers are hired to supervise and counsel a growing inmate population. Expansion and new construction of correctional facilities also are expected to create many new jobs for corrections officers, although state and local government budgetary constraints could affect the rate at which new facilities are built.

Increasing public concern about the spread of illegal drugs resulting in more convictions and the adoption of mandatory sentencing guidelines calling for longer sentences and reduced parole for inmates also will spur demand for corrections officers.

Layoffs of corrections officers are rare because security must be maintained in correctional institutions at all times.

Salaries

According to a 1994 survey in *Corrections Compendium*, a national journal for corrections professionals, starting salaries of state corrections officers averaged about $19,100, ranging from $13,700 in Kentucky to $29,700 in New Jersey. Salaries, overall, averaged about $22,900 and ranged from $17,000 in Wyoming to $34,100 in New York. Salaries generally were comparable for corrections officers working in jails and other county and municipal correctional institutions.

At the federal level, the starting salary was about $18,700 to $20,800 a year in 1995; supervisory corrections officers started at about $28,300 a year. The 1995 average salary for all federal nonsupervisory corrections officers was about $31,460; for supervisors, about $57,100.

Correction officers usually are provided uniforms or an allowance to purchase their own. Most are provided or can participate in hospitalization or major medical insurance plans; many officers can get disability and life insurance at group rates. They also receive vacation and sick leave and pension benefits. Officers employed by the federal government and most state governments are covered by civil service systems or merit boards. In over half of the states, corrections officers are represented by labor unions.

What It's Really Like

Kimberly Diehl—Jailer

Kimberly Diehl is a jailer with the Harris County Sheriff's Department in Houston, Texas.

"In the jail where I work there are four quadrants labeled A through D. Within each quadrant are cell blocks. The cell blocks are where the inmates are actually housed. The jail holds about 12,000 on a daily basis. I'm responsible for about 150. We're the third-largest jail system in the world. "My shift begins at 6:00 A.M. and ends at 2:00 P.M. I enter the FCC (Floor Control Center) booth, where a deputy sits to monitor the sections, inform my sergeant I've arrived, check the roster to see who my partner is, and finally retrieve the keys to my assigned quadrant, which is B quadrant.

"My partner and I then conduct a head count of all the inmates on B quadrant, filling out round sheets as we go. After we finish, the round sheets from the previous shift are tallied and taken to the FCC booth. Each quadrant's deputies will do the same. When all round sheets are in the FCC booth, the deputy will do a count on the entire floor.

"After the floor count, we pick up the inmates' mail and pass it out to them. Also, at this time we must pull out any inmates who are going to the clinic. In addition to the clinic, on any given day, we'll pull out inmates for church, attorney visits, visitation, recreation, bible study, Spanish bible study, hospital visits, school, triage nurse, and court. Some of these activities are spread out on different days; others are done on a daily basis.

"In between doing all this we are required to enter the cell blocks every thirty minutes to check on the inmates. Sometimes we might have to make a special entry because of an argument or a fight. This is also recorded on the round sheet. The round sheet is what would save our rear end if an inmate died on our shift because it tells the time of our entries.

"Our last entry for the day will be around one-thirty in the afternoon. At two o'clock, our shift ends and the evening shift (two to ten) arrives.

"I like the pay, of course. But I also like the shift I work. It gives me all evening to spend with my kids. I work with a good crew of deputies and a great sergeant.

"We have a problem now, though, at work. The air conditioning system isn't working and it's ninety-five degrees outside. This causes a lot of problems with the inmates. They're stuck inside the cell blocks with no air circulation at all. This means a higher risk of their getting into fights. We do have fans on the floors, but all the fans do is circulate the already hot air.

"Another thing I'm not too pleased with is the lack of sick time. When I first hired on in 1990, we were given fifteen sick days to use throughout the year. If you didn't use the sick time it rolled over to the next year. Thus, you could accumulate quite a bit of sick time. Now, we are given three sick hours every payday. So in order to get one day of sick time, it would take a month and half.

"But in spite of the problems, I've found over the years that I could make a difference with the inmates. Not a 180-degree turnaround, mind you. Some of these inmates still come to jail, get out, and then come right back in.

"There are some, though, who are booked into jail, and it's their first time being in any kind of trouble. I try to help them. I'll encourage them to get their GED, for example. The jail provides schooling for those who haven't finished high school. They also have an office practices class and a sewing class. I also try to encourage the drug abusers to sign up for the drug abuse program. It's a very helpful program and there are several who have learned their shortcomings and changed tenfold.

"I see people from all walks of life come through the jail, and to this day I haven't discovered what possesses someone to commit a crime."

How Kim Diehl Got Started

"I began my law enforcement career with the Harris County Sheriff's Department in Houston, Texas, in October 1990. I originally hired on with the sheriff's department for the pay, which is twice what I was making at a bank I worked at.

"After hiring on, I went straight into a two-week training course, which was held inside one of the jail classrooms. In the class they taught us jail procedures and some defensive techniques. We did some role-playing. One of the instructors played the part of an inmate and the other instructor a deputy. We covered a variety of scenarios, such as an inmate threatening to kill himself with a razor or a deputy being attacked while making an enter inside the cell block. What do you do? There are several right answers to these two scenarios, but the most important thing we were told was to think logically.

"A month after the two-week course, we were sent to jail school for a week to get TCLEOSE (Texas Commission on Law Enforcement Officers Standards and Education) certified to work in the jail. This is a tough week, which not only includes eight-hour-a-day class sessions, but also one day devoted to fire school. On this day we are required to put on an air mask and go through a smoke-filled building and search for possible inmates. Upon completion of the week, we are required to take the TCLEOSE test and, of course, we must pass it to continue working. If we don't we go back through the program again."

Expert Advice from Kim Diehl

"My advice for anyone who pursues a career in law enforcement is to make sure you have the right mentality. Also, because the job is so stressful, one needs an 'out,' such as playing tennis, fishing, or just taking a long walk in the evening. One more thing—you must be in good physical shape. It is most assured you will get into a tussle on this job."

CHAPTER TEN

Security Guards

S ecurity guards, also called security officers, patrol and inspect property to protect against fire, theft, vandalism,
and illegal entry. Their duties vary with the size, type, and
location of their employer.

In office buildings, banks, hospitals, and department stores,
guards protect merchandise, money, records, and equipment. In
department stores, they often work with undercover detectives
to watch for theft by customers or store employees.

At ports, airports, and railroads, guards protect merchandise
being shipped as well as property and equipment. They screen
passengers and visitors for weapons, explosives, and other contraband. They ensure that nothing is stolen while being loaded
or unloaded, and they watch for fires, prowlers, and trouble
among work crews. Sometimes they direct traffic.

Guards who work in public buildings, such as museums or art
galleries, protect paintings and exhibits. They also answer routine questions from visitors and sometimes guide tours.

In factories, laboratories, government buildings, data processing centers, and military bases where valuable property or
information such as specifications on new products, computer
codes, or defense secrets must be protected, guards check the
credentials of persons and vehicles entering and leaving the
premises. University, park, or recreation guards perform similar duties and also may issue parking permits or tickets and direct traffic. Golf course patrollers prevent unauthorized persons
from using the facilities and help keep play running smoothly.

At social affairs, sports events, conventions, and other public gatherings, guards provide information, assist in crowd control, and watch for persons who may cause trouble. Some guards work as bouncers and patrol places of entertainment such as nightclubs to preserve order among customers and to protect property.

Armored car guards protect money and valuables during transit. Bodyguards protect individuals from bodily injury, kidnapping, or invasion of privacy.

In a large organization, a security officer often is in charge of the guard force; in a small organization, a single worker may be responsible for all security measures. Patrolling usually is done on foot, but if the property is large, guards may make their rounds by car or motor scooter.

As more businesses purchase advanced electronic security systems to protect their property, more guards are being assigned to stations where they monitor perimeter security, environmental functions, communications, and other systems. In many cases, these guards maintain radio contact with other guards patrolling on foot or in motor vehicles.

Some guards use computers to store information on matters relevant to security, such as visitors or suspicious occurrences during their hours on duty.

As they make their rounds, guards check all doors and windows, see that no unauthorized persons remain after working hours, and ensure that fire extinguishers, alarms, sprinkler systems, furnaces, and various electrical and plumbing systems are working properly. They sometimes set thermostats or turn on lights for janitorial workers.

Guards usually are uniformed and may carry a nightstick and gun, although the bearing of guns is decreasing. They also may carry a flashlight, whistle, two-way radio, and a watch clock, a device that indicates the time at which they reach various checkpoints.

Guards work indoors and outdoors patrolling buildings, industrial plants, and grounds. Indoors, they may be stationed at a guard desk to monitor electronic security and surveillance devices or to check the credentials of persons entering or leaving the premises. They also may be stationed at gate shelters or may patrol grounds in all weather.

Because guards often work alone, there may be no one nearby to help if an accident or injury occurs. Some large firms, therefore, use a reporting service that enables guards to be in constant contact with a central station outside the plant. If they fail to transmit an expected signal, the central station investigates.

Guard work is usually routine, but guards must constantly be alert for threats to themselves and to the property that they are protecting. Guards who work during the day may have a great deal of contact with other employees and members of the public.

Many guards work alone at night; the usual shift lasts eight hours. Some employers have three shifts, and guards rotate to divide daytime, weekend, and holiday work equally. Guards usually eat on the job instead of taking a regular break.

Guards held about 803,000 jobs in 1992. Industrial security firms and guard agencies employed over one-half of all guards. These organizations provide security services on contract, assigning their guards to buildings and other sites as needed. The remainder were in-house guards, employed in large numbers by banks; building management companies; hotels; hospitals; retail stores; restaurants and bars; schools, colleges, and universities; and federal, state, and local governments. Although guard jobs are found throughout the country, most are located in metropolitan areas.

Training

Most employers prefer guards who are high school graduates. Applicants with less than a high school education also can qualify if they pass reading and writing tests and demonstrate competence in following written and oral instructions. Some jobs require a driver's license.

Employers also seek people who have had experience in the military police or in state and local police departments. Most persons who enter guard jobs have prior work experience, although it is usually unrelated. Because of limited formal training requirements and flexible hours, this occupation attracts some persons seeking a second job. For some entrants, retired from military careers or other protective services, guard employment is a second career.

Applicants are expected to have good character references, no police record, good health—especially in hearing and vision—and good personal habits, such as neatness and dependability. They should be mentally alert, emotionally stable, and physically fit in order to cope with emergencies. Guards who have frequent contact with the public should be friendly and personable.

Some employers require applicants to take a polygraph examination or a written test of honesty, attitudes, and other personal qualities. Most employers require applicants and experienced workers to submit to drug screening tests as a condition of employment.

Virtually all states and the District of Columbia have licensing or registration requirements for guards who work for contract security agencies. Registration generally requires that employment of an individual as a guard be reported to the licensing authorities, the state police department, or other state licensing commission. To be granted a license as a guard, individuals generally must be eighteen years old, have no convictions for perjury or acts of violence, pass a background examination, and complete classroom training in such subjects as property rights, emergency procedures, and seizure of suspected criminals. In 1990, only about five states and the District of Columbia had licensing requirements for in-house guards.

Candidates for guard jobs in the federal government must have some experience as a guard and pass a written examination. Armed forces experience also is an asset. For most federal guard positions, applicants must qualify in the use of firearms.

The amount of training guards receive varies. Training requirements generally are increasing as modern, highly sophisticated security systems become more commonplace. Many employers give newly hired guards instruction before they start the job and also provide several weeks of on-the-job training. More and more states are making ongoing training a legal requirement. For example, New York state now requires guards to complete forty hours of training after starting work. Guards receive training in protection, public relations, report writing, crisis deterrence, first aid, drug control, and specialized training relevant to their particular assignment. Guards employed at establishments that place a heavy emphasis on security usually receive extensive formal training. For example, guards at nuclear power plants may undergo several months of training before being placed on duty under close supervision.

Guards may be taught to use firearms, administer first aid, operate alarm systems and electronic security equipment, and spot and deal with security problems. Guards who are authorized to carry firearms may be periodically tested in their use according to state or local laws. Some guards are periodically tested for strength and endurance.

Although guards in small companies receive periodic salary increases, advancement is likely to be limited. However, most large organizations use a military type of ranking that offers advancement in position and salary. Higher-level guard experience may enable persons to transfer to police jobs that offer higher pay and greater opportunities for advancement. Guards with some college education may advance to jobs that involve administrative duties or the prevention of espionage and sabotage. A few guards with management skills open their own contract security guard agencies.

Job Outlook

Job openings for persons seeking work as guards are expected to be plentiful through the year 2005. High turnover and this occupation's large size ranks it among those providing the greatest number of job openings in the entire economy. Many opportunities are expected for persons seeking full-time employment, as well as for those seeking part-time work or second jobs at night or on weekends. However, some competition is expected for the higher-paying in-house guard positions. Compared to contract security guards, in-house guards enjoy better earnings and benefits, greater job security, and more advancement potential, and they are usually given more training and responsibility.

Employment of guards is expected to grow much faster than the average for all occupations through the year 2005. Increased concern about crime, vandalism, and terrorism will heighten the need for security in and around plants, stores, offices, and recreation areas. The level of business investment in increasingly expensive plants and equipment is expected to rise, resulting in growth in the number of guard jobs. Demand for guards will also grow as private security firms increasingly perform duties such as monitoring crowds at airports and providing security in courts formerly handled by government police officers and marshals.

Because engaging the services of a security guard firm is easier and less costly than assuming direct responsibility for hiring, training, and managing a security guard force, job growth is expected to be concentrated among contract security guard agencies.

Guards employed by industrial security and guard agencies occasionally are laid off when the firm at which they work does not renew its contract with their agency. Most are able to find employment with other agencies, however. Guards employed directly by the firm at which they work are seldom laid off because a plant or factory must still be protected even when economic conditions force it to close temporarily.

Salaries

According to a survey of workplaces in 160 metropolitan areas, guards with less responsibility and training had median hourly earnings of $6.00 in 1993. The middle half earned between $5.00 and $7.35 an hour. Guards with more specialized training and experience had median hourly earnings of $11.20, with the middle half earning between $9.05 and $13.34 an hour. Guards employed by industrial security and guard agencies generally started at or slightly above the minimum wage, which was $5.25 an hour in 1996.

Unionized in-house guards tend to earn more than the average. Many guards are represented by the United Plant Guard Workers of America. Other guards belong to the International Union of Guards or the International Union of Security Officers.

Depending on their experience, newly hired guards in the federal government earned between $14,600 and $16,400 a year in 1995. Guards employed by the federal government averaged about $23,300 a year in 1995. These workers usually receive overtime pay as well as a wage differential for the second and third shifts.

What It's Really Like

Timothy T. Speed Jr.—Security Supervisor

Timothy Speed is the security supervisor for a large apartment complex in Oklahoma City, Oklahoma. He has been in this field since 1994.

"Most days are a bit on the boring side. There are many times when you do nothing more than sit, stand, or patrol your post and nothing happens. Then there are days you are so busy you wonder where the time went.

"The atmosphere is mostly quiet on one-officer posts. One-officer posts are those deemed by the powers that be to require only one officer to keep the post secure. These one-officer posts can be anything from warehouses to office buildings with secured entry points, meaning the officer stands or sits at a guard station. Some warehouses have day and night security. The day officer controls the entry point to make sure no unauthorized personnel enter the building, while the night officer ensures the security of the premises by patrolling the interior and exterior for people who might try to break in.

"At most times during the week, our apartment complex is a one-officer post, but during the weekend the post can have as many as three officers on duty.

"Securing an apartment community can be very stressful because we, as security officers, want to keep the peace for the tenants. We are responsible for handling loud noise complaints as well as domestic situations, and these types of calls seem to build, with everything being quiet for months at a time and then the tension breaks and everything goes wild.

"There are times that it can be very dangerous. Some people, who are not the most law-abiding to begin with, think that we security officers don't have the right to tell them what to do. Some of them would just as soon kill you as look at you.

"But really, most of the people are nice. The up side is that you get to meet a lot of people from all walks of life.

"The downside to this work is that there is very little upward momentum, and the pay rate for an armed officer is around $5.50 an hour. With most security agencies I have worked for you are lucky to get minimum wage.

"Here on this job, though, if you work full-time, you get a salary and an apartment. Part-time officers work thirteen hours a week in exchange for an apartment. All officers are required to live on the property in case something big happens."

How Timothy Speed Got Started

"I wanted to do something to help people, and what better way to help people than to make them feel safe in their own homes and office buildings? The first security job I got was through a friend of mine whom I met at the local gun range. She was leaving a position with a security agency to start a job as a corrections officer. I applied and got the job, with my friend's recommendation, of course.

"In Oklahoma, everyone must go through a training program before they can get anything other than a conditional license. I paid for all of my training. After I got my first security job and had my conditional security license, I received training for the unarmed license at the Metro Vo-Tech School in Oklahoma City. This class is forty hours long. You have to have perfect attendance and pass all six tests with an 80 percent score or better.

"I have also received training for certification with an ASP baton, an expandable night stick. In October of 1994 I received training for my armed security officer license. The next month I was trained to carry a semiautomatic pistol. The next year I was trained for the twelve-gauge pump shotgun.

"The armed security license training consists of eight hours of class time and sixteen hours on the firearms range. The automatic pistol training consists of eight hours of range time with the same qualification as the revolver training."

Advice from Timothy Speed

"Firstly, my advice to anyone entering this field is to use the experience as nothing more than a stepping-stone to bigger and better things. A career as a police officer would be a good place to take this. In this field as a security officer you sometimes will be placed in situations that not even some police officers would want to find themselves, and this provides practical experience for any law enforcement position.

"Secondly, always treat the people you will deal with the way you would want to be treated, but also keep them at a distance—because no human being is predictable. In essence, I am saying to treat every person as a possible threat.

"Lastly, if you can help it, never work an unarmed post because the firearm at your side is a great deterrent to would-be criminals. As a safety precaution, I suggest you purchase a bulletproof vest and wear it at all times while on duty.

"Always be alert, even if it's been quiet for months because this is when things start to happen. Always, no matter what the person you are dealing with calls you, keep a professional attitude and perspective on the job. If you let them get to you, you have most definitely lost the battle and let them win.

"And you should realize that most security positions are worked at night, forty hours a week, including weekends, so if you're in this field, be prepared to give up weekends because that is when our job is done."

Professional Associations

F or more information on the careers covered in this book, contact the appropriate professional associations listed below.

Attorneys and Judges

The American Bar Association annually publishes *A Review of Legal Education in the United States*, which provides detailed information on each of the 177 law schools approved by the ABA, state requirements for admission to legal practice, a directory of state bar examination administrators, and other information on legal education. Single copies are free from the ABA, but there is a fee for multiple copies. Free information on the bar examination, financial aid for law students, and law as a career may also be obtained from:

Member Services
American Bar Association
541 North Fairbanks Court
Chicago, IL 60611-3314

Information on the LSAT, the Law School Data Assembly Service, applying to law school, and financial aid for law students may be obtained from:

Law School Admission Services
P.O. Box 40
Newtown, PA 18940

The specific requirements for admission to the bar in a particular state or other jurisdiction may also be obtained at the state capital from the clerk of the state supreme court or the administrator of the state board of bar examiners.

Clerks of the Court

The professional association for clerks of the court is the National Conference of Appellate Court Clerks, which can provide you with career information as well as information about U.S. courts, both trial and appellate.

National Center for State Courts
300 Newport Avenue
P.O. Box 8798
Williamsburg, VA 23187-8798

Court Reporters

For information about shorthand reporting, contact:

National Court Reporters Association
8224 Old Courthouse Road
Vienna, VA 22182

Bailiffs

To learn of job openings, contact the clerk of the court or the chief bailiff in your jurisdiction.

Paralegals

General information on a career as a paralegal and a list of paralegal training programs approved by the American Bar Association may be purchased for $5 from:

Standing Committee on Legal Assistants
American Bar Association
750 North Lake Shore Drive
Chicago, IL 60611

For information on paralegal certification, training programs
in specific states, and standards and guidelines, contact:

National Association of Legal Assistants, Inc.
1601 South Main Street, Suite 300
Tulsa, OK 74119

Information on paralegal careers, schools that offer training
programs, and local paralegal associations can be obtained from:

National Federation of Paralegal Associations
P.O. Box 33108
Kansas City, MO 64114

Information on paralegal training may be obtained from:

American Association for Paralegal Education
P.O. Box 40244
Overland Park, KS 66204

Legal Secretaries

Persons interested in careers as legal secretaries can request
information from:

National Association of Legal Secretaries (International)
2250 East 73rd Street, Suite 550
Tulsa, OK 74136

For general career information, contact:

Professional Secretaries International
10502 NW Ambassador Drive
Kansas City, MO 64195-0404

State employment offices can also provide information about job openings for secretaries.

Law Enforcement Officers

Information about entrance requirements for police work may be obtained from federal, state, and local civil service commissions or police departments.

For information about police work in general, contact:

International Union of Police Associations
1016 Duke Street
Alexandria, VA 22314

Contact any U.S. Office of Personnel Management Job Information Center for pamphlets providing general information and instructions for submitting an application for jobs as U.S. Treasury special agents, drug enforcement agents, or FBI special agents. Look under U.S. Government, Office of Personnel Management, in your telephone directory to obtain a local telephone number.

Private Investigators

For information on a career as a private detective or investigator, contact:

International Security and Detective Alliance
P.O. Box 6303
Corpus Christi, TX 78466-6303

Corrections Officers

Information about entrance requirements, training, and career opportunities for corrections officers may be obtained from the Federal Office of Personnel Management, Federal Bureau of Prisons, state civil service commissions, state departments of correction, or nearby correctional institutions and facilities.

Information on corrections careers, as well as information about schools that offer criminal justice education, financial assistance, and job listings, is available from:

CEGA Services, Inc.
P.O. Box 81826
Lincoln, NE 68501-1826

More information on careers in corrections is available from:

The American Correctional Association
8025 Laurel Lakes Court
Laurel, MD 20707

The American Probation and Parole Association
P.O. Box 201
Lexington, KY 40584

The International Association of Correctional Officers
Box 53
1333 South Wabash Avenue
Chicago, IL 60605

Security Guards

Further information about work opportunities for guards is available from local employers and the nearest state employment service office. Information about registration and licensing requirements for guards may be obtained from the state licensing commission or the state police department. In states where local jurisdictions establish licensing requirements, contact a local government authority such as the sheriff, county executive, or city manager.

About the Author

A full-time writer of career books, Blythe Camenson works hard to help job seekers make educated choices. She firmly believes that with enough information, readers can find long-term, satisfying careers. To that end, she researches traditional as well as unusual occupations, talking to a variety of professionals about what their jobs are really like. In all of her books she includes firsthand accounts from people who can reveal what to expect in each occupation.

Camenson was educated in Boston, earning her B.A. in English and psychology from the University of Massachusetts and her M.Ed. in counseling from Northeastern University.

In addition to *Careers for Legal Eagles*, she has written more than two dozen books for NTC/Contemporary Publishing.